實用
視聽華語
③

PRACTICAL AUDIO-VISUAL
CHINESE

主 編 者◎國立臺灣師範大學國語教學中心
編輯委員◎韓英華・張仲敏・錢進明

正中書局

序

　　中國文化上下五千多年，歷史悠久，博大精深，是中國人在從漁獵採集社會到游牧農業社會一系列發展裡，所孕育出來的文明瑰寶，於世界文化史上，佔有無比重要的地位。時至十九、二十世紀，從一八四○年鴉片戰爭至今一百五十多年間，中國文化受到了來自西方的工業社會及後工業社會的挑戰，開始因應變革、學習調適、檢討反省、轉化創新。

　　尤其是在二次世界大戰後的五十年間，中國人開始分裂成兩個實驗室，各自尋求因應轉化創新之道。第一個實驗室在大陸，可稱之為大陸型導向的中國文化實驗區；另一個在臺灣，可視之為海洋型導向的文化實驗區，任何人，如欲瞭解中國文化在二十世紀的最新發展，必須要對這兩個實驗區裡所產生的成果，細心參考、分析對比，缺一不可。

　　海洋型導向的中國文化，包括臺灣、香港、新加坡……以及全世界有華人聚居的地方，最近十幾年來，尚可包括新進發展的廣州、深圳及大上海地區。總之，海洋型導向的中國文化，傾向自由、開放、多元化的思考模式，社會的發展也兼容並蓄，彈性十足；人們吸收新知快，應變能力強；尊重知識、提倡文教、發展科技、努力人文。相信在二十一世紀，這種文化風格，將推廣至所有華人居住的地方，並進一步產生新的成果，回饋西方社會。

　　而上述理想之實現，其最重要的手段與工具，便是中國語言的學習與推廣。師大國語文中心第六任主任李振清教授有鑑於此，早在民國七十八年，便著手新版國語文教材之策畫與編纂，此一浩大的工程，在國語文中心第七任主任葉德明教授手中，得以完全實現。由葉主任主編，陳惠玲執行編輯，在中心教師陳夜寧、王淑美、盧翠英、范慧貞、劉咪咪、蕭美美、張仲敏、韓英華、錢進明等的通力合作之下，於民國八十三年，厚達千餘頁的《實用視聽華語》三巨冊，終於大功告成，是為當今學習中文的最佳教材。全書內容單元，體例清新，形式及題材充滿了創意，成績斐然，廣獲好評，是目前最受歡迎的華語讀本。

(2)　實用視聽華語㈢

　　然葉主任及編輯群謙沖為懷，並沒有立即將全書正式出版，而以「試用本」的形式問世，希望通過實際教學，吸取各方專家意見，冀能將全書修訂得盡善盡美，以便嘉惠更多的學子。

　　如今，此一修訂本即將由正中書局正式製版付梓，李、葉兩位主任多年的努力，終於完全開花結果。我在此，除了向編者及書局道賀外，也希望藉由此書的正式發行，使海內外所有的專家學者，有機會瞭解此書、使用此書，並提出更進一步的改進之道。同時也希望世界上愛好中華文化的友人，通過此書，能更深刻的瞭解海洋型導向中國文化，並探索其與大陸型中國文化之間，複雜又奧妙的互動關係。

　　畢竟語文只是工具、只是鑰匙；文化才是材料，才是百寶箱，等待我們去不斷琢磨，去時時開啟。

1999 年 8 月

編 輯 要 旨

　　時代在進步，國際間的文化交流也日漸擴充，為了達到彼此間學術研究的目的，學習語文是必要的溝通工具。中華民國教育部有鑑於國內所出版的中文教材已不敷應用 ，而於一九九○年九月委託國立臺灣師範大學國語教學中心編纂「實用視聽華語教材」。

　　本部教材共分《實用視聽華語》㈠、㈡、㈢等三套，每套包括課本、教師手冊、學生作業簿等三冊，每課均附有十分鐘的錄影帶。

　　本書在編寫之初曾邀請國內外專家學者舉行會議，商定編緝計畫、編寫之方式及各冊教材應包括之內容。

　　本書之教法強調以「溝通式」教學為主，因此配合視聽媒體，在每課之前讓學生先看一次錄影帶，引起動機後再進行教學。待學生對於生字、語法、課文、課室活動等全部熟悉後，再看一次錄影帶。此時學生應該對內容完全了解，並說出正確的語言。

　　《實用視聽華語㈠》課本二十五課，重點在訓練學生的基本發音語法及常用字彙，達到語言流利的目的。

　　《實用視聽華語㈡》課本二十八課，偏重大學校園活動和日常生活的話題，介紹文化差異，包括社會、歷史、地理等。語法配合情景介紹句子結構用法，並加上各種不同形式的手寫短文，增加學生識別手寫漢字的能力。

　　《實用視聽華語㈢》課本二十課，課文介紹中華文化之特質及風俗習慣，以短劇、敘述文及議論文等體裁為主，內容包括民俗文化、傳統戲劇、文字、醫藥、科技、環保、消費、休閒等，配合時代潮流，提高學生對目前各類話題討論的能力。

　　本書所有的生字與生詞注音係採用**國語注音符號與漢語拼音**並列，以收廣為使用之效。

　　《實用視聽華語㈠》課本共有生字六百一十四個、生詞八百八十五條；《實用視聽華語㈡》課本共有生字九百個，生詞共計一千三百條；《實用視

(4) 實用視聽華語㈢

聽華語㈢》課本生詞七百二十三條。

　　語法說明係參考耶魯大學教材系統，並按照實際句子情況解釋，在《實用視聽華語㈠》教材中偏重基本句型練習，共有八十九個；《實用視聽華語㈡》教材則以連結結構為重點，共使用二百五十個句型；《實用視聽華語㈢》教材則以書面語之文法為主，介紹文章內所用之文法要點六十七個。

　　每冊教材所包括的內容大致如下：1.課文、對話；2.生字、生詞及用法；3.語法要點及句型練習；4.課室活動；5.短文；6.註釋。《實用視聽華語㈠》及《實用視聽華語㈡》漢字書寫均安排在學生作業中練習。《實用視聽華語㈢》課本中介紹成語及俗語，並附「閱讀與探討」、「佳文欣賞」等項目。

　　本書《實用視聽華語㈠》教材由陳夜寧、王淑美、盧翠英三位老師負責編纂工作；《實用視聽華語㈡》教材由范慧貞、劉咪咪、蕭美美老師等編寫；《實用視聽華語㈢》教材由錢進明、張仲敏、韓英華老師編寫。英文由 Christian A. Terfloth, Robert Kinney; Laura Burian, Earl S. Tai, Michael Fahey, Robert Murphy; Norman Eisley 等人翻譯。插圖由林芳珠、吳昌昇、朱晏臨、吳佳謀、王翰賢、蘇菁瑛等六位畫家完成。

　　本書在編寫初稿完成後，曾邀請國內外學者專家進行審查，經過前後三次修正。審查委員如下：美國夏威夷大學李英哲教授、猶他大學齊德立教授、麻州大學鄧守信教授、柏克萊加州大學張洪年教授、印地安那大學嚴棉教授、麻州衛斯理學院馬靜恆教授、佛羅里達大學屈承熹教授、麻州威廉斯學院顧百里教授、清華大學曹逢甫教授、東海大學馮以堅教授、臺灣師大施玉惠教授、臺灣師大吳國賢教授、臺灣師大羅青哲教授、中華語文研習所何景賢博士。

　　本書之編纂工作費時三年，並進行半年試教及內容修正，感謝所有費心編輯及審核的作者及專家學者，使這部中文教材得以問世，在各位教學者使用後，敬請指正。

葉德明

1999 年 8 月

編 輯 大 意

一、本教材編輯主旨

　　本冊繼第一冊及第二冊後，再加強學習中文之聽、說、讀、寫各方面之能力，並由課文中引介中華文化之特質及風俗習慣等等，以供各大學三、四年級使用。

二、本教材之內容：

　　本書共有二十課，以敘述文及議論文為主，計十七課，另有三課為廣播劇。取材多自報章雜誌，經編輯小組討論後，摘選或改寫，並徵得原作者之同意。所涵蓋之內容十分廣泛，舉凡民俗文化、傳統戲劇、文字、醫藥、科技、環保、消費、休閒等皆包括在內。主題力求清新，且配合時代潮流及日常生活，並面對切身問題，期能激發學生學習之興趣，主動加以討論，進而能將所學靈活運用。

三、本教材之編排每課約分八部分

1. 課文
2. 生詞

3.成語與俗語

4.句型

5.問題討論

6.練習

7.閱讀與探討

8.佳文欣賞

　　為兼具書寫及會話功能，故每課往往以兩種形態文體在1.課文及7.閱讀與探討部分交互出現，俾能引起學生主動會話和討論。有數課附上佳文欣賞以提高學生之閱讀及寫作能力。

四、本教材之相關資料

1.錄 影 帶：以實際生活場景，配合動態畫面，藉視聽教具，讓學生更易明瞭並收到學習效果。教師可在每次上課之前，及每課教學完成之後，各放映一次，引起學生學習動機，並於課後評估學生之理解力。

2.學生作業：配合二十課之課文而寫。幫助學生更加熟悉課文，並能靈活運用所學。

3.教師手冊：提供與課文內容有關的資料，作為老師教學時的參考。

目　錄

第一課　因小失大

劇中人：王美英（英）一位大約二十五歲的小姐
方正浩（浩）王美英的男朋友

英：你窮①按什麼喇叭嘛②！我告訴你多少次了，這是住宅區③，很安靜的，不要亂按④喇叭嘛！

浩：誰叫你動作慢，我等不及啊！

英：我也只不過慢了五分鐘而已。現在都不能等，那以後……

浩：你怎麼沒有戴我送你的手錶啊？

英：哼，你還說呢！你不說手錶我倒忘了，說什麼名牌⑤的手錶，結果啊，兩三天就拋錨⑥了。你看。

浩：拋錨？不會吧？會不會是你不小心把它摔了？或碰到什麼東西了？

英：碰？摔⑦？我看那種手錶不用摔，不用碰，只要三歲的小孩兒用力捏，就會捏⑧碎⑨的。

浩：美英，我花那麼多錢買東西送給你，不喜歡它就算了嘛，何必還諷刺⑩我！

英：我問你，正浩，那隻手錶在哪兒買的？

浩：我在地攤⑪上買的。錶上是名牌標誌⑫，又有保證書⑬，我才

買的。

英：那保證書上蓋了店章⑭沒有呢？

浩：啊！這一點我倒沒有注意到。不過，它的價錢要比普通店裡面賣的便宜一點兒，所以我就……

英：所以你貪⑮它便宜⑯一點，就買下了。

浩：是啊！「貨問三家不吃虧」嘛！

英：哼，我拿那隻錶到店裡修理的時候，錶店的老闆糗⑰了我一頓⑱，說我貪小便宜買了一隻小破爛⑲。哼，起初我以為他還要做我的生意，故意不幫我修理，讓我再買一隻新的。可是後來我連續⑳跑了三家，得到的答案㉑都是一樣的。

浩：美英，對不起嘛！「上一次當，學一次乖」，下一次我再也不敢買地攤上的手錶了。

英：不光是手錶，其他的東西也是一樣的。比較便宜是沒有錯，可是它們要不是仿冒品㉒，就是有瑕疵㉓的。就為了便宜那麼一點點，買到一堆爛東西，不是得不償失嗎？

浩：哎呀，好啦！美英，你不要說這些大道理㉔了，好不好？難得一天的假期，我帶你到郊外去玩玩兒，不要讓手錶的事情，破壞了我們的興緻嘛！

英：好吧，不過最好找一個地方停車，否則車沒地方停，我們也不能下車去玩兒囉！

浩：好，好，一切聽你的。走吧！

一、生詞： New Vocabulary:

1. 窮ㄑㄩㄥˊ qióng

   SV/A: to continuously or exhaustively do something

   她不會來了，你不要窮等了。

   She won't come, you shouldn't keep waiting.

2. 喇ㄌㄚˇ叭ㄅㄚˋ lǎba　**N: (car) horn**

3. 住ㄓㄨˋ宅ㄓㄞˊ區ㄑㄩ zhùzhái qū　**N: residential area**

4. 按ㄢˋ àn

   V:　to press (with the hand or finger), to press (or push) a button

   按了好幾下門鈴，都沒人來開門。

   I pushed the door bell quite a few times, but no one came to open the door.

5. 名ㄇㄧㄥˊ牌ㄆㄞˊ míngpái

   N: a name-brand product, a famous brand of product

6. 拋ㄆㄠ錨ㄇㄠˊ pāomáo

   VO: (a) to cast anchor (of ships)

   　　(b) to become stuck or broken; to get jammed; to stall

   這輛車在路上拋錨了。

   This car is broken on the road.

   這艘船在海上拋錨了。

   This ship is anchored at sea.

7. 摔ㄕㄨㄞ shuāi　**V: to throw, to fling**

他生氣的時候，喜歡摔東西。

When he is angry, he likes to throw things.

8. 捏 niē

V: to pinch, roll or mold between one's fingers

這個捏麵人的手藝真不錯。

This dough-puppet maker's skill is really good.

(In Taiwan and other parts of Asia, dough is often used to sculpt stick puppets. These puppets are often sold on special holidays.)

9. 碎 sùi

V/SV: to break to pieces, smash; to be broken in pieces, smashed

茶杯掉在地上，摔碎了。

A teacup dropped on the ground and shattered.

10. 諷刺 fèngcì　**V/N: to mock, to satirize**

喜歡諷刺別人的人，也會被人諷刺。

People who like to mock others, can themselves be mocked.

11. 地攤 dìtān

N: a streetside vendor, a collection of streetside vendors

12. 標誌 biāozhì　**N: a mark, a symbol, a label**

13. 保證書 bǎozhèngshū　**N: (written) warranty**

14. 蓋章 gàizhāng　**VO: to affix one's seal or stamp**

到銀行取錢的時候要蓋章嗎？

When going to the bank to withdraw money, does one need

to use one's chop?

(An personal stamp or seal in addition to one's signature is required on all official documents in Taiwan. One's name is often carved into a piece of wood or stone and stamped as a seal the documents using red ink. This seal is known as a "chop".)

15. 貪 tān

V: **to have an insatiable desire to do something, to hanker after something, to be tempted to do something**

貪吃貪睡的人一定很胖。

People who have insatiable desires to eat and sleep must surely be quite fat.

16. 便宜 piányí

SV: (**a**) **cheap, inexpensive**

(**b**) **to make cheaper or less expensive**

17. 糗 qiǔ   ***V/SV:*** **to be embarrassed**

我按錯了門鈴，真糗！

I pushed the wrong doorbell, was so embarrassed!

18. 頓 dùn

M: **measure word for a serving of something (meals, criticism, scoldings, beatings, etc.)**

19. 破爛 pòlàn   ***N/AT:*** **junk, waste, refuse, trash**

他是撿破爛的。

He is a junk collector.

20. 連續 liánxù　*A*: in succession, one after another

最近連續發生了五次地震。

Recently there have been five earthquakes in succession.

21. 答案 dáàn　*N*: answer, response

22. 仿冒品 fǎngmàopǐn

　　N: reproduction of a name brand product, imitation of a

　　popular product, a fake

23. 瑕疵 xiácī　*N*: a defect, a flaw

24. 大道理 dà dàolǐ

　　N: a persuasive argument, a high-sounding statement, a lec-

　　ture

二、成語與俗語：Proverbs and Common Sayings:

1. 因小失大 yīnxiǎoshīdà

To lose a big opportunity or gain because of a small consider-

ation. To be penny-wise but pound-foolish.

愛買便宜貨，常常因小失大。

To love buying inexpensive items is often penny-wise but

pound-foolish.

2. 貨問三家不吃虧 huòwènsānjiābùchīkuī

Compare before buying something; shop around before mak-

ing a purchase

你現在別買，貨問三家不吃虧嘛！

You shouldn't buy it now; first go out and compare prices

and quality at other shops.

3. 上一次當學一次乖 shàng yícì dàng xué yícì guāi

Take this as a lesson for next time; learn from a mistake

你被騙了，別生氣，上一次當學一次乖。

You've been cheated, don't get angry, just take this as a lesson for next time.

4. 得不償失 débùchángshī

The loss outweighs the gain; not worth the effort or price

貪便宜買到假貨，真是得不償失。

The inclination to buy inexpensive yet false goods is really a waste of one's money.

三、句型： Sentence Patterns:

1. 只不過……而已

to only be, to just be (i.e., to only cost......, to just be asking......)

(1) 這隻手錶只不過五百元而已，真便宜。

(2) 我只不過問問價錢而已，並不真想買。

(3) 今天只不過熱一點而已，濕度並不高。

2. ……不用……，只要……就……了

......don't need to......, only need to......then......it will be (enough, satisfactory)

(1) 你不用來等我，只要告訴我是哪個住宅區就可以了。

(2) 你現在不用說，只要到時候提醒我就好了。

(3) 你不用去，只要打個電話給他就行了。

3. ⋯⋯就算了，何必還⋯⋯

⋯⋯then that's fine, there is no need to still......

(1) 你不買就算了，何必還諷刺我。

(2) 你不做就算了，何必還跟他吵。

(3) 你不吃就算了，何必還倒掉。

4. 不光是⋯⋯，其他⋯⋯

It is not just......, there are other(s)......

It is not only......, there are other(s)......

(1) 不光是你，其他的同學也不懂。

(2) 不光是這個問題，其他幾個問題也還沒解決呢！

(3) 不光是我不贊成，其他的人也有意見。

四、問題討論： Questions for Discussion:

1. 方正浩為什麼亂按汽車喇叭？

_____

2. 方正浩怎麼會在地攤買錶？

_____

3. 你買東西喜歡買便宜貨嗎？為什麼？

_____

4. 「因小失大」這句成語在本課是什麼意思？

_____

五、你怎麼辦？ What would you do?

1. 如果有人在你住家附近亂按喇叭⋯⋯

_____

2. 如果你的男（女）朋友送你一隻假錶……

_____

3. 如果老闆不給你修理假錶……

_____

4. 如果你找不到地方停車……

_____

六、練習：Practice Exercises:

1. 配字：（意思相同的連起來）

Match the words(connect words or phrases of the same meanings):

⑴ 拋錨	A. 冒牌貨
⑵ 保證書	B. 被騙一次得一次經驗
⑶ 連續	C. 譏笑
⑷ 上一次當學一次乖	D. 擔保書
⑸ 窮按	E. 一連
⑹ 瑕疵	F. 毛病
⑺ 諷刺	G. 回答
⑻ 糗了我一頓	H. 壞了，停了
⑼ 答案	I. 按個不停
⑽ 仿冒品	J. 說得我好沒面子

2. 接句 (Complete the sentences)：

例：你不說我倒忘了，__你一說我就想起來了__。

Example: If you hadn't mentioned it I would have forgotten, but now that you mention it I remember.

⑴ 誰叫你動作慢，我_____。

(2) 現在都不能等，那結婚以後 ＿＿＿＿＿＿＿ 。

(3) 這是住宅區，＿＿＿＿＿＿＿＿＿ 。

(4) 不喜歡就算了，何必 ＿＿＿＿＿＿＿＿ 。

(5) 錶是名牌，所以 ＿＿＿＿＿＿＿＿＿ 。

(6) 這破錶三歲小孩兒用力捏，＿＿＿＿＿＿＿ 。

(7) 不光是手錶，其他 ＿＿＿＿＿＿＿＿＿ 。

(8) 買到一堆爛東西，不是 ＿＿＿＿＿＿＿ 嗎？

(9) 不要讓這件事，破壞了 ＿＿＿＿＿＿＿ 。

(10) 如果找不到地方停車，我們也不能 ＿＿＿＿ 。

3.分辨詞義：（選合適的填入）

Differentiate the meanings of the following:

(1) 安　靜　頑皮的孩子忽然＿＿靜下來，一定是有病了。

清　靜　學文學的女生看起來很＿＿靜。

文　靜　老年人喜歡＿＿靜，獨自一個人過日子。

(2) 等不及　你再不用功就＿＿不及趕上同班同學的進度了。

來不及　她朋友還沒來接，她已經＿＿不及先走了。

趕不及　快點，飛機半個鐘頭就要飛了，不然＿＿不及登機了。

(3) 貪便宜　＿＿便宜的人，只可能一二次，朋友認清了，就遠離他了。

佔便宜　有的太太買菜的時候，喜歡＿＿便宜，可是買的菜不新鮮。

小便宜　千萬別接受朋友給的＿＿便宜，可能他要你幫忙。

(4) 連　續　他＿＿學了三年的中文，沒有停過。

不　斷　她學中文學了一年停了，後來又＿＿學了一年。

繼　續　學中文必須＿＿地練習，才有好成績。

(5) 答　案　老師問學生一個問題，學生＿＿了以後，老師很滿意。

答　覆　他打電話來請我們立刻＿＿他的要求。

回　答　這部分的考題＿＿都在書後頭。

4.擴大應用語功能：

Expand your vocabulary:

(1) 我告訴你多少次了。

我跟你說了好幾遍了。

我不是已經跟你說過了嗎？

(2) 不喜歡它就算了嘛，何必還諷刺我。

不喜歡它就別要嘛，何必還說氣人的話。

不喜歡它就還給我，何必還譏笑我。

(3) 這一點我倒沒有注意到。

這方面我倒沒留意到。

你說的這問題我倒沒想到。

(4) 得到的答案都是一樣的。

都這麼說。

回答一模一樣。

(5) 比較便宜是沒錯。

便宜一點是真的。

真比別的便宜。

(6) 不是得不償失嗎？

不是白花了錢了嗎？

不是花了錢沒買到好東西嗎？

第二課　拒①吸二手煙②

　　有些煙癮③大的人，早上一起床就點一根煙來吸，說是能提神醒腦；辦公時吸煙，說是能提高工作效率④；寫作時吸煙，說是能招來靈感⑤；煩惱⑥時吸煙，說是能消愁解悶；娛樂⑦時吸煙，說是能增加樂趣⑧。更常常把「飯後一根煙，賽過⑨活神仙⑩」掛在口上。抽煙真有這些好處嗎？還是他們自我安慰，把它拿來當作不願戒煙⑪的藉口⑫呢？

　　吸煙污染空氣，易引起火災⑬，這是人人皆知的。而根據醫學人士證明，吸煙促成⑭的疾病如癌症⑮、肺氣腫⑯、氣管炎⑰等等，不論吸煙者或吸入二手煙者，都有同等程度的染患機會，這真使人震驚⑱。吸煙者若得了這些疾病，無話可說，怨不得⑲別人。不吸煙的人，因別人吸煙使空氣污濁⑳，被迫㉑吸入大量「尼古丁」㉒而得了這些病，實在冤枉㉓，真是太不公平㉔了。

　　在目前的環境中，到處可見販賣㉕香煙的地方，而香煙的廣告更是生動㉖、富吸引力㉗。煙商㉘贊助㉙各種體育活動，更令年輕一代迷惑㉚而養成吸煙的壞習慣。

　　我們要站起來，大聲呼籲㉛「拒吸二手煙」。辦公室、電梯㉜內、火車、汽車裡都嚴禁㉝吸煙；公共場所嚴格㉞規定㉟

「非㊱吸煙區㊲」和「吸煙區」。若有違規㊳吸煙者，人人都應該勇敢㊴地去制止㊵他。對於下一代年輕人要多做勸導㊶工作，灌輸㊷他們正確㊸的知識，以維護㊹他們的健康㊺，防止㊻吸煙族㊼的日漸㊽猖獗㊾。

　　總之，我們要多方努力，才能達到「拒吸二手煙」的目的。

一、生詞：New Vocabulary:

1. 拒 jù　*V*: **to refuse, to reject**

   她拒收我送給她的禮物。

   She refused to accept the gift I gave to her.

2. 二手煙 èrshǒuyān

   N: **second-hand smoke（smoke one breathes as the result of someone else's cigarette smoking）**

3. 癮 yǐn　*N*: **an addiction, a craving, an urge**

4. 效率 xiàolǜ　*N*: **efficiency**

5. 靈感 línggǎn　*N*: **inspiration**

6. 煩惱 fánnǎo

   V/N: **(*a*) to be worried, to be vexed, to be troubled**

   　　　(*b*) worries, cares

   你在煩惱什麼？

   What are you worrying about?

7. 娛樂 yúlè

   N/AT: **an amusement, an entertainment, a recreation**

8. 樂趣 lèqù　*N*: a pleasure, an enjoyment, a joy

9. 賽過 sàiguò　*V*: to exceed, to surpass, to overtake

她美得賽過天上的仙女。

Her beauty exceeds that of Xiān Nǚ (in the heavens).

(Xiān Nǚ is a legendary character who lives in heaven. She is an immortal of great beauty.)

10. 活神仙 huóshénxiān　*N*: immortal

11. 戒煙 jièyān　*VO*: to give up smoking

有人說戒煙不難，他已經戒了一百次了。

Someone (once) said that to give up smoking wasn't hard, he had already given it up a hundred times.

12. 藉口 jièkǒu　*N*: an excuse, a pretext

13. 火災 huǒzāi　*N*: a fire (as a disaster)

14. 促成 cùchéng　*V*: to help bring about, to help cause

共同的利益促成兩國的合作。

Common interests helped to bring about the two countries' co-operation.

15. 癌症 yánzhèng　*N*: cancer

16. 肺氣腫 fèiqìzhǒng　*N*: lung inflammation, emphysema

17. 氣管炎 qìguǎnyán　*N*: bronchitis

18. 震驚 zhènjīng　*V*: to astonish, to shock, to amaze

愛滋病的發現震驚了全世界。

The discovery of AIDS shocked the entire world.

19. 怨不得 yuànbùdé

***IE*: cannot blame, cannot put the blame on**

字寫不好怨不得別人，只能怨自己懶。

One cannot blame others for writing characters poorly; one can only blame one's own laziness.

20. 污ㄨ濁ㄓㄨㄛˊ wūzhuó

***AT*: (of air, water, etc.) dirty, filthy, muddy**

污濁的空氣影響健康。

Dirty air affects one's health.

21. 迫ㄆㄛˋ pò　　***V*: to force, to compel, to press**

他被迫加入黑社會。

He was forced to join the underworld (a criminal organization).

22. 尼ㄋㄧˊ古ㄍㄨˇ丁ㄉㄧㄥ nígǔdīng　　***N*: nicotine**

23. 冤ㄩㄢ枉ㄨㄤˇ yuānwǎng

***V/N*: to wrong (someone), to treat unjustly**

我沒拿你的東西，別冤枉我。

I didn't take your things; don't treat me unjustly (by making this accusation). You wrong me by accusing me of taking your things.

24. 公ㄍㄨㄥ平ㄆㄧㄥˊ gōngpíng

***SV/AT*: to be fair, just, impartial, equitable**

父母對兒女要公平，老師對學生也必須公平。

Parents should be fair to their sons and daughters; teachers must also be impartial with their students.

25. 販ㄈㄢˋ賣ㄇㄞˋ fànmài　***V*: to sell, to peddle**

街上到處都有販賣機，販賣果汁、香煙、報紙等。

On the street there are vending machines everywhere, selling fruit juice, cigarettes, newspapers, etc.

26. 生ㄕㄥ動ㄉㄨㄥˋ shēngdòng

***SV/AT*: to be lively, vivid, eye-catching**

她畫的人物很生動。

The characters in her paintings are very lively.

27. 吸ㄒㄧ引ㄧㄣˇ力ㄌㄧˋ xīyǐnlì　***V*: attraction, fascination**

28. 煙ㄧㄢ商ㄕㄤ yānshāng

***N*: the cigarette business, the cigarette industry**

29. 贊ㄗㄢˋ助ㄓㄨˋ zànzhù

***V/N*: to sponsor, to support, to patronize**

請贊助我們拒吸二手煙的活動吧！

Please support our movement against second-hand smoke!

30. 迷ㄇㄧˊ惑ㄏㄨㄛˋ míhuò

***V/N*: to misguide, to delude, to confuse**

不要受壞人的迷惑。

Don't misguided by bad people

31. 呼ㄏㄨ籲ㄩˋ hūyù

***V/N*: to (formally) call for (action, efforts, etc.), to appeal for, to petition**

她大聲呼籲開車的人要注意交通安全。

She loudly appealed for drivers to pay attention to traffic

safety.

32. 電梯 diàntī　*N*: **an elevator**

33. 嚴禁 yánjìn　*V*: **to strictly forbid, to strictly prohibit**

工廠嚴禁煙火。

The factory strictly prohibits (the lighting of) fires.

34. 嚴格 yán gé　*SV/AT*: **to be strict, rigid**

從前父親管小孩很嚴格。

In the past fathers were very strict with their children.

35. 規定 guīdìng

V/N: (***a***) **to stipulate**

(***b***) **rule(s), regulation(s)**

按照學校的規定，在教室裡不可吸煙。

According to the school regulations, one cannot smoke in the classrooms.

36. 非 fēi　*BF*: **not, no, cannot**

37. 吸煙區 xīyānqū　*N*: **smoking area**

38. 違規 wéigūi

VO: **to be against regulations, to violate rules, to break laws, illegally**

他常常違規停車，被罰了不少錢。

He often parks illegally and has been fined quite a bit of money.

39. 勇敢 yǒnggǎn　*SV/AT*: **to be brave, courageous**

英雄都是聰明勇敢的人。

Heroes are all smart and courageous people.

40. 制止 zhìzhǐ　　**V/N: to stop, halt, curb**

看見別人有不正當的行為，你敢去制止嗎？

When you see people behaving improperly, do you dare to stop them?

41. 勸導 quàndǎo　　**V/N: to exhort and guide, to advise**

小孩不想念書，父母應該勸導，不可以打罵。

When a child doesn't want to study, parents should exhort and guide him, not beat and scold him.

42. 灌輸 guànshū　　**V: to instill into, to imbue with**

不良的書籍常常灌輸讀者錯誤的觀念。

Poor books often imbue their readers with false ideas.

43. 正確 zhèngquè

　　SV/A: to be accurate, correct; appropriate, proper

他的發音很正確。

His pronunciation is very accurate.

44. 維護 wéihù　　**V: to defend, to uphold, to protect**

維護健康的辦法就是多運動、吃適量的食物。

The way to protect one's health is to exercise more and eat the right amount of food.

45. 健康 jiànkāng　　**N: health**

46. 防止 fángzhǐ　　**V: to prevent, to guard against, to avoid**

為了防止日曬，出門一定要戴帽子或打傘。

In order to avoid a sunburn, when going outdoors one should

wear a hat or carry a parasol（umbrella）.

47. 吸煙族 xīyānzú　*N*: **smokers, people who smoke**

48. 日漸 rìjiàn　*A*: **with each passing day, day by day**

愛吸煙的人日漸減少，愛打電動玩具的人日漸增多。

The number of people who love smoking is decreasing day by day; while the number of people who love playing electronic games is increasing with each passing day.

49. 猖獗 chāngjué　*SV/N*: **rampant, unbridled, run wild**

現在小偷猖獗，應想辦法對付。

Presently petty thievery is running rampant; a way should be thought of to deal with it.

二、成語與俗語：Proverbs and Common Sayings:

1. 提神醒腦 tíshénxǐngnǎo

   to arouse and stimulate; to invigorate and keep the mind clear

   喝茶可以提神醒腦。

   Drinking tea can arouse and stimulate（a person）.

2. 消愁解悶 xiāochóujiěmèn

   to eliminate sorrow and dissipate worry, to cheer up

   跟朋友聊天可以消愁解悶。

   Talking to a friend can cheer one up.

3. 自我安慰 zìwǒ ānwèi

   to comfort oneself, to console oneself, to reassure oneself

   「船到橋頭自然直」是自我安慰的話。

"A boat which comes to a bridge must go straight"

is a saying to reassure oneself.

*（The saying "A boat which comes to a bridge must go straight" creates the image of a boat which must steer clear of the supports of the bridge, the two shores, and whatever rocks may lay in its path by allowing the current to draw it straight ahead. Thus, the meaning is: Things will take care of themselves when the time comes.）

三、句型：Sentence patterns:

1. 若有……應該……

If there is......then one should......

If there are......then one ought to......

(1) 若有不排隊買票的人，我們應該去制止他。

(2) 若有意見，應該提出來討論。

(3) 若有不認識的字，應該查字典。

2. 不論……（都）有同等

No matter whether it is（X or Y）......they all have the same......,

No matter......they all have the same......

(1) 不論男人或女人，都有同等的受教育機會。

(2) 不論東方人或西方人，都有同等的學習能力。

(3) 我院子裡不論什麼花，都有同等的生長空間。

3. 要……才能

X must......then X can......

X will need to......then X will be able to

(1) 你要不斷努力，才能學好中文。

(2) 我們要合作，才能達到目的。

(3) 他要改掉壞習慣，才能找到好工作。

四、問題討論：Questions For Discussion:

1. 談談吸煙和吸入二手煙的害處。

　　　　　　　　　　　　　　　　　　　

2. 政府可用哪些方法來防範吸煙族的猖獗？

　　　　　　　　　　　　　　　　　　　

3. 愛吸煙的人易得什麼病？

　　　　　　　　　　　　　　　　　　　

4. 談談你自己吸煙、戒煙的經驗。

　　　　　　　　　　　　　　　　　　　

5. 談談你對青少年吸煙的看法。

五、練習：Substitution Exercises:

1. 填空：喝咖啡，聽音樂，做早操，約好友作伴，不聊天。

Use the phrases above to fill in the blanks.

(1) 早上一起床就　　　　　　　　，說是能提神醒腦。

(2) 辦公時　　　　　　　，說是能提高工作效率。

(3) 寫作時　　　　　　，說是能招來靈感。

(4) 煩惱時　　　　　　，說是能消愁解悶。

(5) 娛樂時　　　　　　，說是能增加樂趣。

2.課文複習：

Vocabulary review:

例：吸煙污染空氣，這是人人皆知的。

Example: Smoking pollutes the air; this is something everybody knows.

(1) 吸煙易引起＿＿＿＿＿＿，這是人人皆知的。

(2) 吸煙促成疾病如＿＿＿＿＿、＿＿＿＿＿、＿＿＿＿＿這是人人皆知的。

(3) 吸煙吸入大量＿＿＿＿＿，這是人人皆知的。

(4) 香煙廣告生動，令年輕人＿＿＿＿＿，這是人人皆知的。

(5) 辦公室、電梯內、火車、汽車裡＿＿＿＿＿，才能達到「拒吸二手煙」的目的。

(6) 公共場所嚴格規定＿＿＿＿＿和＿＿＿＿＿，才能達到「拒吸二手煙」的目的。

(7) 若有違規吸煙者＿＿＿＿＿，才能達到「拒吸二手煙」的目的。

(8) 對於下一代年輕人＿＿＿＿＿，＿＿＿＿＿才能達到防止吸煙族的日漸猖獗。

佳文欣賞

———禁煙與賣煙———

何　凡

暑假期間見到許多位從美國來臺的親友，發現他們不分男

女老幼，都有一種「反煙」的共識。有的人說他已經戒了。有的人相約到陽臺上過癮，而不在主人屋中點火。大學生層的青年則說學校裡現在不流行吸煙，因為煙害的強烈已經確定，他們不願意自己到名成業就的中年時期被煙打倒。大家的共同說法是，美國政府與民間合作，規定公共場所及交通工具上，包括飛機國內航線一律禁煙；餐廳闢一角為「吸煙區」，煙客坐在那裡吞雲吐霧，自覺與眾不同，也頗乏味。甚至機關主管在自己的辦公室裡也不能吸煙，理由是免得二手煙有害進室談公事的部下。像這樣的「百般刁難」，視煙客為人民公敵，煙客既然動輒得咎，足以壓迫他們萌生戒除的決心。對於躍躍欲試的青少年也具有嚇阻的力量。據報載，美國近十年來，吸煙人口已減少了百分之四十，使美國的煙草行業受到嚴重的打擊。

　　美國煙不在臺灣報紙電視上登廣告，六年的工夫就搶去臺灣香煙專賣市場的百分之六十的生意，恐怕沒有其他商品有這樣大的魔力。愛吸美煙的以青年學生為多，臺灣的美煙經銷商也為青少年舉辦集會，進行推銷。賣煙賣酒最好以青年為對象，因為他們一上癮就是一輩子的主顧，他們的心、肺等器官受過尼古丁的毀損，即使中途戒除，已受的傷害恐怕也難完全去除。故此反煙的釜底抽薪之計是從青少年下手，讓他們根本不落入吸煙的圈套，這比協助已經入套的人脫套，可以事半而功倍。勸導青少年禁煙最佳的人選是他們的家長和老師，如有家長老師因為自己抽煙而無法啟齒，則趁機戒自己更有一舉兩

得之妙。萬一辦不到這件事，亦無妨現身說法，告訴子弟煙癮易上難除，自己就是榜樣，最好是根本不入煙門或是及早戒除，可以一輩子享受不盡。因為現在雖然醫學發達，對於煙害仍舊無計可施。故此青少年諸君應當珍惜自己的錦鏽前程，不要早期自投香煙羅網，以致到輝煌中年時被閻王爺從電腦上收賬。

～原載於《中央日報》1993.3.31～

問答：Answer the following question:

1. 為什麼作者自美來臺的親友有「反煙」的共識？

_____

2. 美國如何實行禁煙？禁煙的結果如何？

_____

3. 美煙在臺灣如何推銷？

_____

4. 作者認為應該如何禁煙？

_____

5. 作者如何勸勉青少年遠離香煙？

_____

第三課　活到老學到老

　　人的一生，要經過幾個不同的教育階段①，有學前、幼稚、小學、中學、大學、研究所教育。由於時代的進步，除了一般正規②教育外，教育學者也一再強調③成人教育、終身④教育的重要性。

　　很多人以為學校教育是教育唯一⑤的來源⑥，其實，家庭和社會對教育的影響都很大。父母是兒女的第一位老師，父母的一言一行，都是兒女學習的榜樣⑦。兒女在入學以前，家庭就是他們的學校。社會的動態⑧，形形色色看在或聽在青少年眼裡、耳裡，都會形成正面⑨或負面⑩的教育意義。學校教育全是經過設計規畫⑪的教材，理論⑫多於實際⑬。剛出校門的人，不明白其中的差別⑭，會迷失⑮於社會的多變之中。

　　過去老師或父母教什麼，我們就學什麼，對老師或父母有過多的依賴⑯。今天教育的意義是教育一個人懂得如何教育自己，他才能獨立自主，真正做一個人。

　　人生的成就⑰是多方面的，成績絕不是唯一的目標⑱。一個對自己有信心，時時保持旺盛⑲鬥志⑳的人，必有成就。教育的目的，在教導一個人如何負責㉑盡職㉒、尊重㉓自己、尊重別人

的成就。學業成績雖然很重要，而人格教育更重要。

俗語說：「活到老學到老。」完成學校的教育以後，踏入社會，更要不斷地學習，不斷地吸收新知，以充實㉔自己，提升自己，這樣才能應付這多變的社會，工作時才能得心應手，活得快樂，活得有意義、有價值。

一、生詞：New Vocabulary：

1. 階段 jiēduàn *N*: stage (s), phase (s)

2. 正規 zhènggūi *AT*: standard; regular; orthdox

   職業訓練可補正規教育的不足。

   Occupational training can make up for deficiencies of standard education.

3. 強調 qiángdiào *V*: to stress, to emphasize

   老師常常強調內在美的重要。

   Teachers often stress the importance of inner beauty.

4. 終身 zhōngshēn *N*: all one's life, life-long

   結婚是一個人的終身大事。

   Marriage is one of the major events in one's life.

5. 唯一 wéiyī *AT*: the only one, the only kind

   爸爸是我唯一的親人。

   Father is my only (living) relative.

6. 來源 láiyuán *N*: source, origin

7. 榜樣 bǎngyàng *N*: model, role-model, good example

8. 動態 dòngtài *N*: tendency, trends, developments

9. 正面 zhèngmiàn *N/AT*: positive (aspect)

10. 負面 fùmiàn *N/AT*: negative (aspect)

11. 規畫 guīhuà *V/N*: to plan; scheme

市政府正在細心規畫一個森林公園。

The city government is in the midst of carefully planning a public forest.

12. 理論 lǐlùn *N*: theory

13. 實際 shíjì

SV/N/AT: (*a*) practical, realistic

(*b*) reality, practice

實際的行動勝過空想。

Realistic action is superior to idle dreaming.

14. 差別 chābié *N*: a difference, a disparity

貴公司女職員的待遇有沒有差別？

Is there a difference in the way women office workers are treated in your company?

15. 迷失 míshī *V/AT*: to lose (one's way, etc.), to be lost

現在有些年輕人說他們是迷失的一代。

Nowadays some young people say they are a lost generation.

16. 依賴 yīlài *V*: to depend on, to rely on

孩子大了以後，就不要再依賴父母了。

Once children have grown up, they shouldn't rely on their parents any more.

17. 成就 chéngjiù

N: achievement, accomplishment, success

18. 目標 mùbiaū　*N*: goal, target, aim, objective

19. 旺盛 wàngshèng

SV/AT: to be productive, prosperous, vigorous; high（morale）

旺盛的精力是開創事業的基本條件之一。

Productive energy is one of the most fundamental factors in the undertaking of a cause.

20. 鬥志 dòuzhì

N: fighting spirit, morale, the determination to compete or fight

他雖然失敗了，鬥志還很旺盛。

Although he lost he is still exuberantly determined to fight.

21. 負責 fùzé

SV/V: (*a*) to be conscientious, responsible

(*b*) to be in charge of, to be responsible for

(*a*) 他做事很負責。

He works very conscientiously.

(*b*) 請你負責這方面的工作。

Will you please take charge of this part of the job?

22. 盡職 jìnzhí

AT/SV/VO: to do one's duty, to have a sense of responsibility

負責盡職的人到處受歡迎。

People who conscientiously do their duty are welcome

everywhere.

23. 尊ㄗㄨㄣ重ㄓㄨㄥ zūnzhòng　**V/N: respect, esteem**

尊重別人的人也會受到別人的尊重。

Those people who respect others will receive the respect of others (in return).

24. 充ㄔㄨㄥ實ㄕ chōngshí

SV/V: (a) abundant, substantial

(b) to strengthen or improve (knowledge, facilities, etc.); to enrich

(a) 這本書的內容很充實。

The contents of this book are very substantial.

(b) 我們要多多充實自己的知識。

We want to really enrich our knowledge.

二、成語與俗語： Proverbs and Common Sayings:

1. 活ㄏㄨ到ㄉㄠ老ㄌㄠ學ㄒㄩㄝ到ㄉㄠ老ㄌㄠ huódào lǎo xuédào lǎo

there is still much to learn after one has grown old; the pursuit of knowledge is an endless effort.

每個人都要活到老學到老。

Each and every person should make the pursuit of know-ledge an endless effort.

2. 一ㄧ言ㄧㄢ一ㄧ行ㄒㄧㄥ yìyányìxíng

Everything one says and does; one's words and actions

我們的一言一行都要謹慎，不可隨便。

We must be careful in everything we say and do; we mustn't be careless.

3. 形形色色 xíngxíngsèsè

of every description; of all shapes and colors; of great variety and diversity

大學裡有很多形形色色的社團。

In the University there are a great variety and diversity of organizations.

4. 得心應手 déxīnyìngshǒu

to handle with ease; to be in one's element

他勤練書法已經五年了，所以寫起來得心應手。

He has already diligently studied calligraphy for five years; therefore he is in his element (he feels at ease) when writing.

三、句型：Sentence Patterns:

1. ……以為……其實……

......mistakenly believe......actually......

......wrongly believe......in truth......

(1) 大家以為他很窮，其實他很有錢。

(2) 我以為外面下雨，其實是大晴天。

(3) 她以為種玫瑰花很容易，其實很難。

2. ……多於……

......X outnumbers Y......

The are more X than Y

(1) 世界上小國多於大國。

(2) 社會上好人多於壞人。

(3) 坐公車上學的多於走路的。

3. ⋯⋯V.什麼⋯⋯V.什麼

......VERB whatever it is, then......VERB whatever it is

......VERB whatever, then......VERB whatever.

(1) 你做什麼，我就吃什麼。

(2) 你喜歡穿什麼，你就穿什麼。

(3) 他的女朋友叫他學什麼，他就學什麼。

4. ⋯⋯如何⋯⋯才能⋯⋯

......how to......then......

......what to......then......

(1) 他不知道如何學中文，才能學得好。

(2) 他不知道如何說，才能使別人相信她。

(3) 我們要如何努力，才能達到世界和平？

5. 雖然⋯⋯而⋯⋯

......although......however......

......though......but......

(1) 一個人的工作能力雖然重要，而品德更重要。

(2) 生命雖然重要，而自由更重要。

(3) 食物雖然重要，而飲水更重要。

四、問題討論：Questions for Discussion:

1. 請依次說出五個不同的教育階段。

_____

2. 除了一般正規教育外還有什麼教育也很重要？

_____

3. 學校教育和現實社會有什麼差別？

_____

4. 教育的意義是什麼？

_____

5. 人格教育為什麼比學業成績重要？

_____

6. 為什麼俗語說：「活到老學到老」？

_____

7. 你贊成不贊成父母或老師體罰孩子？為什麼？

_____

五、練習：Practice Exercises:

1. 配句：

Match the phrases:

(1) 人生要經過不同的教育
階段，_____

(2) 學業成績雖然很重要，

_____

A. 都是兒女學習的榜樣。

B. 理論多於實際。

(3) 學校教育是經過設計規　　　　C. 他才能獨立自主。
　　畫的教材，_____

(4) 父母的一言一行，　　　　　　D. 有學前、幼稚園、小
　　　　_____　　　　　　　　　學、中學、大學、研究
　　　　　　　　　　　　　　　　　所等教育。

(5) 一個人懂得如何教育自　　　　E. 而人格教育更重要。
　　己，_____

2.將生詞連成句子：

Use each of the following to create a sentence:

例：　　唯一
　　　　學校　　　　｝　學校是唯一吸收新知的地方。
　　　　吸收

　　(1) 正規
　　　　強調　　　　｝　_____
　　　　進步

　　(2) 負責
　　　　成就　　　　｝　_____
　　　　信心

　　(3) 得心應手
　　　　旺盛　　　　｝　_____
　　　　目標

　　(4) 形形色色
　　　　迷失　　　　｝　_____
　　　　多變的

(5) 依賴
 　獨立 ｝＿＿＿＿＿＿＿＿＿＿＿＿＿
 　榜樣

3.改錯：

Correct the errors in the sentences:

(1)有學前、幻稚、小學、中學、研就所。 ＿＿＿

(2)家廷和社會對教育的影嚮都很大。 ＿＿＿

(3)過去我們對父母和老師有過多的依懶。 ＿＿＿

(4)一個人如何負責盡織，遵重自己和別人。 ＿＿＿

(5)踏入社會，更要不繼地學習，不繼地吸受新知。 ＿＿＿

第四課　不經一事不長一智

　　林琳從十二歲起就嚮往①歐洲，她看過很多介紹歐洲的雜誌和書籍，歐洲的美麗風光與著名古蹟②深深地吸引著她。今年夏天她已經大學畢業兩年了，終於下定決心，把銀行的存款③提出來，報名④參加了一個遊歐洲的旅行團。在二十天的旅程中要遊八個國家的觀光勝地⑤，行程非常緊湊⑥。

　　在旅程中的第三天晚上，大家坐在露天⑦音樂座⑧上聆聽⑨音樂演奏⑩。當華爾滋⑪美妙⑫的旋律⑬使人如醉如痴時，她突然發覺放在腿上的皮包不翼而飛了。這真是一個晴天霹靂，在皮包裡有錢和比錢更重要的護照，怎麼辦呢？這時她已無心聽音樂，內心焦急⑭萬分，好不容易等到音樂會結束了，她告訴領隊⑮和其他團員，大家推測⑯也許竊賊⑰取出皮包裡的錢後，會把皮包連同護照丟在附近，所以大家分頭在座位下面、樹下、草叢⑱裡、垃圾桶⑲內尋找，結果徒勞無功，只好回到當晚住宿的旅館。

　　第二天一大早，旅行團就要出發到另一個目的地旅遊，她必須獨自⑳留下來，團員們都來安慰她，並借給她一些錢，使

她內心感到很溫暖。但大家走後，頓時，懊惱㉑、惶恐㉒、孤寂㉓、淒涼㉔、茫然㉕無助的感覺一起湧㉖上心頭，好不容易等到上班時間，領隊找的一位住在當地的張先生來旅館協助她，這時她的心才好過了一點兒。

張先生首先㉗帶她去警察局去報了案㉘，再去拍快照，補辦㉙護照，然後到英法領事館去補辦簽證。大概因為當時是旅遊旺季㉚吧，每個地方都是大排長龍㉛，等一切都辦妥之後，已是下午五點了。他們趕忙去坐火車，趕到下一站的旅館。她想如果沒有張先生的帶領，那真是寸步難行。到了旅館，團員們都圍上來慰問她，她像和失散的家人團聚一般地流下了既辛酸㉜又快樂的眼淚……。

現在她早已安全返國，只要聽說有朋友出國旅遊，她就會一再叮嚀㉝朋友，護照和錢千萬要放在貼身㉞口袋裡，另外不要忘了要帶幾張像片和一點急救㉟藥品㊱。

一、生詞：New Vocabulary

1. 嚮往 xiàngwǎng　*V*: to aspire to; to long for

   她一直嚮往田園生活。

   She has always aspired to an idyllic life.

2. 古蹟 gǔjī　*N*: historic site(s), place(s) of historic interest

3. 存款 cúnkuǎn　*N*: savings (in a bank)

4. 報名 bàomíng

   VO: to sign up, enter one's name, register, enroll

這次的旅行你報名了嗎？

Have you signed up for the trip this time?

5. 勝地 shèngdì　**N: famous scenic spot, famous landmark**

6. 緊湊 jǐncòu

　　SV/AT: to be well organized; to be tightly packed

　　晚會的節目很緊湊。

　　The program for this evening's banquet is very well organized.

7. 露天 lùtiān　**AT: outdoors, open-air**

8. 音樂座 yīnyuèzuò　**N: auditorium, music hall**

9. 聆聽 língtīng　**V: to listen (attentively or respectfully)**

　　他在樹下聆聽鳥叫。

　　He stood beneath the tree listening to the birds singing.

10. 演奏 yǎnzòu

　　V: to give an instrumental performance, to perform (for musi-cians)

　　你剛才演奏的是什麼曲子？

　　What song did you just perform?

11. 華爾滋 huáěrzī　**N: a waltz**

12. 美妙 měimiào

　　SV/AT: to be beautiful, splendid, wonderful

　　她覺得人生太美妙了，真不明白為什麼每年有那麼多人自殺？

　　She feels that life is beautiful; she really cannot understand why so many people commit suicide each year.

13. 旋律 xuánlǜ　*N*: **melody**

14. 焦急 jiāojí　*V*: **to be worried, anxious, anxiety- ridden**

現在已經晚上八點了，小孩還沒回來，父母焦急萬分。

Now it is already eight o'clock in the evening. The child still has not returned, and the parents are extremely worried.

15. 領隊 lǐngduì　*N*: **the team leader, the group leader**

16. 推測 tuīcè

V/N: **to guess; to make a conjecture, to infer; to predict**

據他推測，明年物價會下降。

According to his guess, commodity prices will drop next year.

17. 竊賊 qièzéi　*N*: **a thief, a burglar**

18. 草叢 cǎocóng　*N*: **brush, clumps of grass**

19. 垃圾桶 lājītǒng/lèsètǒng

N: **a garbage can, a trash can**

20. 獨自 dúzì　*N*: **alone, personally, single-handedly**

21. 懊惱 àonǎo

SV/AT: **to be upset; to be annoyed; to be vexed**

考試時看錯了題目，他很懊惱。

He was very upset when he studied the wrong topic for the test.

22. 惶恐 huángkǒng

SV/AT: **to be terrified, to be frightened**

我懷著一顆惶恐的心去面試。

I had terror in my heart as I went to face the interview.

23. 孤寂 gūjí *SV/AT*: **to be lonely**

沒有家的老人太孤寂了。

Old people without families are too lonely.

24. 淒涼 qīliáng

SV/AT: **to be miserable; to be desolate and sorrowful; to be lonely**

戰爭過後，戰場上的景象很淒涼。

After the war, the battlefield was a desolate scene.

25. 茫然 mángrán

SV/A: **to be perplexed; to be confounded; to be ignorant; to be in the dark**

我問他一個數學問題，他一臉茫然。

When I asked him an arithmetic problem, he looked totally perplexed.

26. 湧 yǒng *V*: **to well (up), to spring (forth)**

清涼的泉水不斷的湧出來。

Cool and refreshing spring water continuously sprang forth.

27. 首先 shǒuxiān *A*: **first, in the first place, first of all**

第一次出國的人首先要辦護照。

People going abroad for the first time should first arrange for a passport.

28. 報案 bàoàn

VO: to report a case to the police (such as a theft, a murder or a missing person)

有人被殺了，趕快報案！

A person has been murdered; notify the police at once!

29. 補辦 bǔbàn　　*V*: to replace

證件遺失了必須補辦。

Lost credentials must be replaced.

30. 旺季 wàngjì

N: (said of business) the busy season, the boom season

31. 排長龍 pái chánglóng

IE: To have long lines, to have to wait in long lines, to have to cue up, to have to line up

32. 辛酸 xīnsuān　　*SV*: to be miserable, to be bitter, to be sad

他不喜歡別人提起他的辛酸往事。

He does not like other people to bring up his sad memories.

33. 叮嚀 dīngníng　　*V/N*: to urge, to exhort repeatedly

媽媽一再叮嚀我開車前不要喝酒。

Mother has repeatedly urged me not to drink alcohol before driving.

34. 貼身 tiēshēn

AT: (*a*) (to glue to one's body) to keep closely attached, to keep carefully on or by one's person

(*b*) personal servant(s)

重要的政治人物都有貼身隨從。

Important government officials always have personal servants (bodyguards) accompanying them.

35. 急ㄐㄧ救ㄐㄧㄡ jíjiù *AT/V*: **first-aid, emergency treatment**

這個病人的心臟病發了，醫生正在急救。

This patient just had a heart attack and the doctor is now giving him first-aid.

36. 藥ㄧㄠ品ㄆㄧㄣ yàopǐn *N*: **medicine**

二、成語與俗語： Proverbs and Common Sayings:

1. 不ㄅㄨ經ㄐㄧㄥ一ㄧ事ㄕ不ㄅㄨ長ㄓㄤ一ㄧ智ㄓ bùjīngyíshìbùzhǎngyízhì

If one does not go through an experience, then one cannot gain knowledge; one learns by experience

「不經一事不長一智」是告訴我們經驗的重要。

(The saying) "If one does not go through an experience, one cannot gain knowledge" tells us how important experience is.

2. 如ㄖㄨ醉ㄗㄨㄟ如ㄖㄨ痴ㄔ rúzuìrúchī

to be crazy about; to fall head over heels in love with; to be drunk with

她的歌聲甜美，使聽眾如醉如癡。

Her singing voice is so sweet that it made the (listening) audience crazy about her.

3. 不ㄅㄨ翼ㄧ而ㄦ飛ㄈㄟ búyìérfēi

to vanish; to melt into thin air; to disappear mysteriously

我的手錶不翼而飛了。

My wristwatch vanished.

4. 晴天霹靂 qíngtiānpīlì

a bolt from the blue, a great and sudden shock, a completely
unexpected occurrence

有人告訴他，他家的房子倒了，真是晴天霹靂。

Some people told him that his house had collapsed; it was
really a great shock to him.

5. 徒勞無功 túláowúgōng

all one's attempts proved futile; to labor in vain; to work without achieving anything

汽車的輪胎陷到坑裡去了，大家忙了半天徒勞無功。

The tire of the car got stuck in a hole; everbody spent a long
time (trying to get it out) but their attempts proved futile.

6. 寸步難行 cùnbùnánxíng

unable to move a single step; hard to walk even an inch

這個城市交通太亂，使人寸步難行。

The traffic in this city is so disordered, that it makes it hard
for people to walk even an inch.

三、句型： Sentence Patterns:

1. 首先……再……然後

......first (do something)......then (do something else)......then
after that (do a third thing)......

(1) 他回家後，首先洗手、洗臉，再喝茶，然後做功課。

(2) 有好吃的東西時，首先給父母，再給兄弟姐妹，然後給鄰居。

(3) 看報時，我首先看國內外大事，再看國際大事，然後看運動新聞。

2. 如果……那真是

If......that really is......

If......, then that really would be......

(1) 如果你能幫我忙，那真是太好了。

(2) 如果我像鳥一樣能飛，那真是太高興了。

(3) 如果我能得第一，那真是開心極了。

四、問題討論：Questions for Discussion:

1. 林琳是怎麼去歐洲的？行程是怎麼安排的？

_____

2. 皮包是什麼時候掉的？為什麼她焦急萬分？

_____

3. 第二天她獨自留下來有什麼感覺？什麼時候才覺得舒服一點？

_____

4. 張先生帶她去哪兒？辦了什麼事？她怎麼和其他團員會合？

_____

5. 「不經一事不長一智」是什麼意思？

_____

6. 你去過哪些地方旅行？印象最深刻的是哪兒？

_____

7. 當你旅行時你最注意或觀察哪一方面的事物？

_____

8. 你喜歡一人或是結伴去旅行？為什麼？

_____

9. 當你旅行時有沒有上當或受騙的經驗？

_____

五、練習 ： Practice Exercises:

1. 選擇相反詞 ：

Underline the word with the opposite meaning:

例：存款： 　　　　*a.*提款　 *b.*放款　 *c.*儲蓄

(1)緊湊： 　　　　*a.*要緊　 *b.*鬆散　 *c.*緊張

(2)露天： 　　　　*a.*天空　 *b.*室內　 *c.*露營

(3)分頭： 　　　　*a.*分開　 *b.*比較　 *c.*一起

(4)旺季： 　　　　*a.*淡季　 *b.*雨季　 *c.*四季

(5)團聚： 　　　　*a.*團結　 *b.*會面　 *c.*分散

(6)辛酸： 　　　　*a.*歡樂　 *b.*安慰　 *c.*勞累

(7)安全： 　　　　*a.*平安　 *b.*危險　 *c.*全部

(8)首先： 　　　　*a.*第一　 *b.*以後　 *c.*最後

(9)獨自： 　　　　*a.*自己　 *b.*大家　 *c.*獨立

(10)結束： 　　　　*a.*開始　 *b.*結果　 *c.*協助

2. 分辨 ：

Differentiate the two characters:

(1) 嚮、響　你受了誰的影＿＿來學中文？

　　　　　他因＿＿往中華文化，喜歡看中國畫。

(2) 籍、藉　愛買書的人，書房裡的書＿＿＿堆成山。

　　　　　學生常常找＿＿＿口，不來上課。

(3) 遊、游　參加團體活動，得先知道他們的＿＿＿戲規則。

　　　　　＿＿＿泳是年輕人最喜愛的運動。

(4) 奏、秦　在演＿＿＿會上，人人都靜靜地聆聽。

　　　　　萬里長城是＿＿＿朝時完成的。

(5) 旋、旅　去一次歐洲＿＿＿費不便宜。

　　　　　坐在＿＿＿轉椅上，玩的人都笑呵呵。

(6) 霹、避　打雷了，＿＿＿靂一聲，嚇死人啦！

　　　　　大雨時，我們躲在屋內＿＿＿雨。

(7) 賊、則　偷東西的人就是＿＿＿。

　　　　　他對人對事都有原＿＿＿。

(8) 徒、待　做事得先計畫，不然＿＿＿勞無功。

　　　　　剛畢業的學生，找的工作＿＿＿遇都不高。

(9) 惱、腦　他＿＿＿羞成怒，怨別人。

　　　　　＿＿＿力強的人有思考能力。

(10) 孤、狐　動物中＿＿＿狸是最聰明的。

　　　　　無父母的孩子是＿＿＿兒。

(11) 旺、枉　旅行＿＿＿季買不到機票。

　　　　　不要冤＿＿＿好人。

(12) 辛、幸　他＿＿＿苦了一生，總算成功了。

　　　　　運氣好的人真＿＿＿福。

閱讀與探討
Read and Discuss

導遊自白

　　我是一名頗富經驗的導遊。在大學主修歷史，畢業後即失業。在百般無奈下，擠入導遊這一行業。藉工作的機會，高山大川，名勝古蹟……都有我的足跡。五年多跑下來，居然迷上了這份「不務正業」的工作。帶旅行團出發，安排旅館，接洽土產店……這些繁雜瑣碎的工作，實在有不少令人稱奇的甘苦談。

　　首先我談談我工作的對象。按年齡來說是包括老、中、青各級男女人士。身為導遊須先訓練了解各色人等的談話資料。我會迎合年輕人唱搖滾樂，也會跳迪斯可；我能跟少、壯、中年人大談流行服飾；我更會與老年團員狂吹養生之道。不簡單吧！因此我也交到了不少知心的朋友。

　　其次，我得有敏銳的觀察力，必須隨時注意每位團員的反應。如有人落落寡歡，得前去搭訕一番，不知有什麼不滿意的事；如有人精神不好，又得詳加細問是否身體不適；如有男女團員相互傾心，我還得藉機會當一次月下老人，從中撮合撮合呢！當一名導遊，觀察力強是必要的條件啊！也不簡單吧！

　　最後，我認為最苦的事是歷史念多了，古蹟看多了，在娓

娓講述介紹名勝古蹟的時候，常說溜了嘴，張冠李戴了呢！

　　告訴你一件最得意的事。有一次帶一團老人去半日遊，遊完下車的時候，第一位老太太給了我一點小費，隨後每人都照樣給了小費，結果那一天我就有筆額外的收入，真是意想不到的好運氣！你想從事導遊的工作嗎？歡迎你參加我們的行列。

問答：Answer the following questions:

1. 大學畢業生哪些科系的學生比較容易找工作？

_____

2. 做導遊必須有哪些條件？譬如體健、有口才……？

_____

3. 你認為組織旅行團，一定要分年齡、職業……不同性質嗎？

_____

4. 旅行時最怕發生哪些問題？

_____

5. 「愛之船」的旅行真能撮合不少傾心的少男少女嗎？為什麼？

_____

6. 你認為導遊工作適合你的興趣嗎？如果你要加入這行列，你有什麼新「點子」？

_____

佳文欣賞

瑞　士

朱自清

　　瑞士有「歐洲的公園」之稱。起初以為有些好風景而已：到了那裡，才知無處不是好風景，而且除了好風景似乎就沒有什麼別的。這大半由於天然，小半也是人工。瑞士人似乎是靠遊客活的，只看很小的地方也有若干、若干的旅館就知道。他們拼命地築鐵道通輪船，讓愛逛山的愛遊湖的都有落兒；而且車船兩便，票在手裡，愛怎麼走就怎麼走。瑞士是山國，鐵道依山而築，隧道極少，所以老是高高低低，有時相差得很遠的。還有一種爬山鐵道，這兒特別多，狹狹的雙軌之間，另加一條特別軌：有時是一個個方格兒，有時是一個個鉤子。車底下帶一種齒輪似的東西，一步步咬著這些方格兒，這些鉤子，慢慢地爬上爬下。這種鐵道不用說工程大極了，有些簡直是筆陡筆陡的。

　　逛山的味道實在比遊湖好。瑞士的湖水一例是淡藍的，真正平得像鏡子一樣。太陽照著的時候，那水在微風裡搖晃著，宛然是西方小姑娘的眼。若遇著陰天或者下小雨，湖上迷迷濛濛的，水天混在一塊兒，人如在睡夢裡。也有風大的時候；那時水上便皺起粼粼的細紋，有點像顰眉的西子。可是這些變

幻的光景在岸上或山上纔能整個兒看見，在湖裡倒不能領略許多。況且輪船走得究竟慢些，常覺得看來看去還是湖，不免也膩味。逛山就不同，一會兒看見湖，一會兒不看見：本來湖在左邊，不知怎麼一轉彎，忽然挪到右邊了。湖上固然可以看山，山上還可看山，阿爾卑斯山有的是重巒疊嶂，怎麼看也不會窮。山上不但可以看山，還可以看谷；稀稀疏疏錯錯落落的房舍，彷彿有雞鳴犬吠的聲音，在山肚裡，在山腳下，看風景能夠流連低迴固然高雅，但目不暇接地過去，新境界層出不窮，也未嘗不淋漓痛快；坐火車逛山便是這個辦法。

～《歐遊雜記》～

第五課　世界運動會

　　四年一次的世界運動會是件全球矚目①的大事。各國選手②無不摩拳擦掌，渴望③在大會中奪④得錦標⑤與光榮⑥。

　　世界運動會也稱為國際⑦奧林匹克⑧運動會⑨。遠在兩千多年前，古代希臘⑩人在希臘北部一個叫做奧林匹亞⑪的地方，集合⑫各城邦⑬舉行每四年一次的祭祀⑭儀式⑮，在典禮⑯過程中，加入一些競技比賽活動。本來的目的是以和平與友愛的精神，來消弭⑰各城邦之間的仇視⑱與戰爭⑲。相傳⑳下來，形成了現在的國際奧林匹克世界運動大會的組織㉑。這個國際性的組織是在十九世紀㉒末才成立的。由於在廢墟㉓中發現了奧林匹克遺址㉔，不少熱心體育的教育人士，他們貢獻㉕出畢生㉖的精力㉗，於一八九六年在希臘雅典㉘舉行了第一屆㉙國際奧林匹克大會，也簡稱㉚為奧運會。此後沿襲㉛傳統㉜，每四年舉行一次。一九九二年是第二十五屆，選在西班牙㉝的巴塞隆納㉞大規模㉟正式揭幕㊱。

　　世界性的體育活動應該是象徵㊲著全人類㊳的和諧㊴共處與團結㊵合作。由會旗㊶上的五環㊷，就可以會意㊸到大會的主旨㊹——使世界上五大洲的人，不分種族㊺，不分國籍㊻，同沐㊼在

「世界大同，天下一家」的氣氛中。但是近年來有些人因政治恩怨[48]，藉大會舉行期間，製造不少暴亂[49]恐怖[50]事件，令人惋惜[51]。

人人深切[52]盼望[53]，這轟動[54]全球的大競技[55]活動，永遠給我們帶來幸福、歡樂與進步。

一、生詞：New Vocabulary:

1. 矚目 zhǔmù

   V/AT: to watch or stare at with great interest, to eagerly look at, to take great interest in

   選舉總統是全國矚目的大事。

   The entire nation watches the event of the presidential election with great interest.

2. 選手 xuǎnshǒu

   N: candidate; (of sports) selected contestant or player

3. 渴望 kěwàng　**V: to yearn for, to thirst for, to long for**

   孩子們都渴望著暑假的來臨。

   The children all long for the arrival of summer vacation.

4. 奪 duó

   V: (a) to strive for, to win

   (b) to take by force, to seize

   他的皮包被別人奪走了。

   His briefcase was forcibly taken by someone.

5. 錦標 jǐnbiāo　**N: a trophy, a prize, a title**

6. 光榮 guāngróng　*N/AT/SV*: honor, glory, credit

7. 國際 guójì　*AT*: international

8. 奧林匹克 àolínpīkè　*P/N*: Olympic

9. 運動會 yùndònghùi　*N*: games, sports meet

10. 希臘 xīlà　*PN*: Greece

11. 奧林匹亞 àolínpīyǎ　*PN*: Olympia

12. 集合 jíhé　*V/AT*: to gather; to assemble; to call together

明天早上八點，在我們學校大門口集合。

Gather at our school's main gate tomorrow morning at 8 am.

13. 城邦 chéngbāng　*N*: city-state

14. 祭祀 jìsì

V: to worship; to honor by a service or rite; to offer sacrifices

祭祀祖先是中國人的傳統。

Ancestor worship is a Chinese tradition.

15. 儀式 yíshì　*N*: a ceremony, a rite

16. 典禮 diǎnlǐ　*N*: a ceremony, a celebration

17. 消弭 xiāomǐ

V: to terminate; to put an end to; to bring to an end

消弭種族間的仇恨是很多國家努力的目標。

Putting an end to racial hatred is a goal many nations are working hard to achieve.

18. 仇視 chóushì

V/N: to look upon with hatred; to regard with hostility; to

be hostile to

不同種族的人若彼此仇視，就無法團結合作了。

When people of different races bitterly look upon each other with hatred, then there is no way for them to cooperate with each other.

19. 戰爭 zhànzhēng　*N*: war; warfare

20. 相傳 xiāngchuán

V: to hand down from generation to generation; to pass on from one to another

這種風俗是一代一代相傳下來的。

This custom has been passed down from generation to generation.

21. 組織 zǔzhī

V/N: (*a*) to organize

(*b*) an organization

他們想組織一個新的政黨。

They want to organize a new political party.

22. 世紀 shìjì　*N*: century

23. 廢墟 fèixū　*N*: the ruins (of a city, a castle, etc.)

24. 遺址 yízhǐ　*N*: the ruins (of a city, a castle, etc.); the relics

25. 貢獻 gòngxiàn

V/N: (*a*)to contribute; to devote; to dedicate

(*b*)a contribution

這位醫生為尋求一種醫治的方法而貢獻一生。

The doctor dedicated his life to finding a cure.

26. 畢生 bìshēng

A: all one's life, throughout one's lifetime; lifelong

她畢生從事教育工作。

She has been involved in education all her life.

27. 精力 jīnglì　　**N: energy, stamina, vigor**

28. 雅典 yǎdiǎn　　**N: Athens (the capital of Greece)**

29. 屆 jiè

MA: measure word for periods of time or events (meetings, sports events, etc.)

你是本校第幾屆畢業生？

With which class (what year) did you graduate from this school?

30. 簡稱 jiǎnchēng

V/N: (a) to be called something for short

(b) an abbreviation, a shortened form of a name

山東省的簡稱是魯。

Shandong Province's abbreviation is "Lu".

(NOTE: All of the Chinese provinces have abbreviated names of one character. These abbreviated names can be found in a number of dictionaries.)

31. 沿襲 yánxí

V: to follow; to carry on as before; to follow old or traditional (customs, practices, etc.)

一國的政治制度是沿襲舊的好？還是創新的好？

Is it best for a country to carry on with the practices of its old political system or to create a new one?

32. 傳統 chuántǒng　*N/AT*: **a tradition, a convention**

33. 西班牙 xībānyá　*PN*: **Spain**

34. 巴塞隆納 bāsàilóngnà　*PN*: **Barcelona**

35. 大規模 dàguīmó　*AT*: **massive, large-scale, expansive**

這家工廠舉行大規模的產品展覽會。

This factory held a massive product exhibition.

36. 揭幕 jiēmù

V: **to unveil (a monument, etc.); to open (a meeting, exhibition, etc.)**

今年的世運會什麼時候揭幕？

When is the opening of this year's Olympics?

37. 象徵 xiàngzhēng　*V/N*: **to symbolize; to signify**

登陸月球象徵人類能征服自然。

The moon landing signifies that humanity can conquer nature.

38. 人類 rénlèi　*N*: **humanity, mankind**

39. 和諧 héxié

AT/SV/N: **(a) to be in harmony, harmonious, (b) harmony**

(a) 這兩種聲音在一起很和諧。

These two sounds are very harmonious together.

(b) 鄰居們相處得很和諧。

The neighbors get along very harmoniously.

40. 團結 tuánjié　*V/N*: **to rally together, to unite**

要想戰勝敵人必須團結起來。

If we want to defeat the enemy, we must unite.

41. 會旗 huìqí　*N*: **the flag of a club or organization**

42. 五環 wǔhuán

PN: **five rings (i.e., the five linked rings which are the symbol of the Olympic games)**

43. 會意 huìyì　*V*: **to understand the meaning, to take a hint**

我暗示他兩次，他都不能會意，只好明白地告訴他了。

I have already given him a hint twice, but he just is not taking the hint. The only way to make him understand is to tell him.

44. 主旨 zhǔzhǐ

N: **the theme; the main point (of a speech, statement, etc.)**

45. 種族 zhǒngzú　*N/AT*: **race, ethnic race**

46. 國籍 guójí

N: **nationality; national background; citizenship**

47. 同沐 tóngmù

V: **to mutually refresh; to go through a group catharsis; to share a cleansing experience; to bathe in together**

這位老師很和氣，使全班學生同沐於春風中。

That teacher is very kind, he is making the whole class share the refreshment of the spring breeze.

48. 恩怨 ēnyuàn

N: a feeling of gratitude; a feeling of resentment; gratitude or grudge

49. 暴亂 bàoluàn　　*N*: **a rebellion; a revolt**

50. 恐怖 kǒngbù　　*SV/AT*: **terror; fear; horror**

恐怖電影常常令女孩子尖叫。

Horror films often make girls scream.

51. 惋惜 wànxī　　*V/AT/SV*: **to feel regret over something**

已經過去的事就不必惋惜了，我們應該向前看。

One mustn't feel regret over things which have already happened, we should look forward (towards the future).

52. 深切 shēnqiè　　*A*: **profound, heartfelt**

有子女以後，才深切體會到父母的愛心。

Only after having a son or a daughter, can one profoundly understand parental love.

53. 盼望 pànwàng

V: **to hope for; to look forward to; to long for**

在寒冷的冬天裡，人們盼望著春天的到來。

In the midst of icy winter people long for the arrival of spring.

54. 轟動 hōngdòng

V: **to cause a sensation, to cause a stir**

足球比賽本校得到第一名，轟動全國。

This school took first place in the football tournament and it caused a stir throughout the country.

55. 競技 jìngjì　*N*: **sports, athletics**

二、成語與俗語：Proverbs and Common Sayings:

1. 摩拳擦掌 móquáncāzhǎng

to be eager for a fight or to compete; to get ready for a fight; to be eager to start on a task; to chafe at the bit

比賽前選手們都在摩拳擦掌，希望奪得第一名。

Before the competition all of the competitors are eager for a fight; they all hope to win first place.

2. 世界大同，天下一家 shìjièdàtóng, tiānxiàyìjiā

universal brotherhood with all people as one family under heaven

你想如何才能達到「世界大同，天下一家」的理想呢？

How do you think it would be possible to achieve the dream of "universal brotherhood with all people as one family under heaven"?

三、句型：Sentence Patterns:

1.……以……，來……

......(to) do.......in order to.......

......to do X......in order to Y......

(1) 她常常以跳舞唱歌來娛樂自己和家人。

(2) 他每天以慢跑來鍛練身體。

(3) 工人們常常以不工作（罷工）來要求加薪。

2. 藉……製造

......to use......in order to......

......to use（as an excuse）......for the chance to......

(1) 他常常藉生病製造和女朋友見面的機會。

(2) 有些人藉開會期間製造暴亂。

(3) 有人藉問問題製造認識對方的機會。

四、問題討論：Questions for Discussion:

1. 會旗上五環有什麼意義？

_____

2. 國際奧運會本來的目的是什麼？後來呢？

_____

3. 近年來舉行的世界運動會期間有什麼令人惋惜的事？

_____

4. 世界運動會有沒有在貴國舉行過大會？你有沒有親自參觀？

_____

五、練習：Practice Exercises:

1. 課文複習：

Vocabulary Review:

(1) 世界運動會是件全球_____的大事。

(2) 各國選手無不_____，渴望在大會中奪得

_____與_____。

(3) 古希臘人在希臘北部一個叫做＿＿＿＿＿＿＿＿的地方，集合各城邦舉行＿＿＿＿＿＿＿年一次的＿＿＿＿＿＿儀式。

(4) 一九九二年是第＿＿＿＿＿＿＿屆，選在＿＿＿＿＿＿的巴塞隆納大規模正式揭幕。

(5) 世界性的體育活動應該是象徵著全人類的＿＿＿＿＿＿＿共處與＿＿＿＿＿＿＿合作。

(6) 會旗上的五環代表世界上＿＿＿＿＿＿＿的人。

(7) 希望世界上的人，不分＿＿＿＿＿＿＿，不分＿＿＿＿＿＿，同沐在「世界＿＿＿＿天下＿＿＿＿」的氣氛中。

2.造句：

Make Sentences:

(1) 無不：＿＿＿＿＿＿＿＿＿＿＿＿＿＿＿＿＿＿＿

(2) 集合：＿＿＿＿＿＿＿＿＿＿＿＿＿＿＿＿＿＿＿

(3) 消弭：＿＿＿＿＿＿＿＿＿＿＿＿＿＿＿＿＿＿＿

(4) 仇視：＿＿＿＿＿＿＿＿＿＿＿＿＿＿＿＿＿＿＿

(5) 和諧：＿＿＿＿＿＿＿＿＿＿＿＿＿＿＿＿＿＿＿

(6) 盼望：＿＿＿＿＿＿＿＿＿＿＿＿＿＿＿＿＿＿＿

3.選同音字：

Choose the character with the same sound and tone:

例：世：　　　a.史　b.事　c.石　d.十

　(1) 奧：　　　a.興　b.舉　c.傲　d.襖

　(2) 臘：　　　a.辣　b.獵　c.拉　d.鼠

　(3) 儀：　　　a.以　b.議　c.義　d.遺

　(4) 祭：　　　a.幾　b.季　c.登　d.及

⑸ 邦：　　　　a.幫　b.旁　c.部　d.棒

⑹ 祀：　　　　a.次　b.司　c.四　d.己

⑺ 傳：　　　　a.船　b.傅　c.專　d.川

⑻ 壚：　　　　a.許　b.續　c.居　d.須

⑼ 揭：　　　　a.節　b.接　c.姐　d.借

⑽ 旨：　　　　a.只　b.隻　c.直　d.至

4.填空：

Use the following to fill in the blanks:

競技　競賽　競選　競爭

⑴ 羅馬的_____場很大。

⑵ 工商業_____得很激烈。

⑶ 本校每年都參加龍舟_____。

⑷ 你參加明年的國會議員_____嗎？

遺址　遺失　遺書　遺忘

⑴ 他把過去不愉快的事都_____了。

⑵ 他自殺了，家人找到了三封_____。

⑶ _____護照者必須補辦。

⑷ 古代奧運會的_____在哪裡？

舉手　舉止　舉行　舉一反三

⑴ 明天本校_____運動大會。

⑵ 贊成明天去旅行的人請_____。

⑶ 能_____的人，必是聰明人。

⑷ 他的_____很文雅。

團圓　團體　團結　團團圍住

⑴ _____就能產生力量。

(2) 中秋節是全家_____的日子。

(3) _____票比較便宜。

(4) 這位電影明星，一下飛機，就被記者_____了。

驚天動地　驚醒　驚人　驚訝

(1) 昨天夜裡發生大地震，_____了全家人。

(2) 這個小孩會說英、法、德、日語真令人_____。

(3) 他希望有一天能做一件_____的事。

(4) 他每天吃十個蛋真_____。

閱讀與探討
Read and Discuss

世運會開幕典禮

　　第二十五屆世運會在開幕典禮以前，大會決定用箭把火射到聖火臺上，點燃聖火。這個決定引起各界的爭論。傳統的方式是選一名身強力壯的運動員持火把到聖火臺上去點燃聖火。有些人認為這種以箭引火的方式雖然很吸引人，有古典味道，可是太冒險了。如果箭手因緊張而有失誤的話，必定引起觀眾的譁然，有損開幕典禮的莊嚴，因此建議大會仍用傳統方式，或改採其他方式，但被大會拒絕。

　　誰擔任這個冒險的任務呢？大會一直不對外宣布，直到點燃聖火時才知道是位殘障運動員，名叫雷伯洛，今年三十七歲，西班牙馬德里人，曾在 1984 年紐約、1988 年漢城世運殘

障運動員比賽中獲射箭銅牌。

　　在這次開幕典禮上，大家緊張地等待著，手上捏了把冷汗，結果他不負眾望，一箭中的，全場歡聲雷動，給大會揭開了空前的、漂亮的序幕。

問答：Answer the following questions:

1. 用箭怎樣把聖火點燃？

_____

2. 傳統的點燃聖火方式是怎麼樣的？

_____

3. 用箭點燃聖火為什麼令人擔心？

_____

4. 用箭點燃聖火的雷伯洛得過什麼獎牌？

_____

5. 他在這次開幕典禮上的表現怎麼樣？

_____

佳文欣賞

運動家的風度

羅家倫

　　提倡運動的人，以為運動可以增加個人和民族體力的健康。是的，健康的體力，是一生努力成功的基礎；大家體力不

發展，民族的生命力也就衰落下去。

　　古代希臘人以為「健全的心靈，寓於健全的身體」。這也是深刻的理論。身體不健康，心靈容易生病態，歷史上、傳記裡和心理學中的例證太多了。

　　這些都是對的；但是運動的精義，還不只此。它更有道德的意義，這意義就是在運動場上養成人生的正大態度、政治的光明修養，以陶鑄優良的民族性。這就是我所謂「運動家的風度」。

　　養成運動家的風度，首先要認識「君子之爭」、「君子無所爭，必也射乎。揖讓而升，下而飲，其爭也君子。」這是何等光明、何等雍容。運動是要守著一定的規律，在萬目睽睽的監視之下，從公開競爭而求得勝利的：所以一切不光明的態度，暗箭傷人的舉動，和背地裡佔小便宜的心理，都當排斥。犯規的行動，雖然可因此得勝，且未被裁判者所覺察，然而這是有風度的運動家所引為恥辱而不屑採取的。

　　有風度的運動家，要有服輸的精神：「君子不怨天，不尤人。」運動家正是這種君子。按照正道做，輸了有何怨尤。我輸了只怪我自己不行：等我充實改進以後，下次再來。人家勝了，是他本事好，我只有佩服他；罵他不但是無聊，而且是無恥。歐美國家的人民，因為受了運動場上的訓練，服輸的精神是很豐富的。這種精神，常從體育的運動場上，帶進了政治的運動場上。譬如這次羅斯福與威爾基競選，在競選的時候，雖

然互相批評，但是選舉揭曉以後，羅斯福收到第一個賀電，就是威爾基發的。這賀電的大意是：我們的政策，公諸國民之前，現在國民選擇你的，我竭誠地賀你成功。這和網球結局以後，勝利者和失敗者隔網握手的精神一樣。此次威爾基失敗以後，還幫助羅斯福作種種外交活動：一切以國家為前提，這也是值得贊許的。

有風度的運動家，不但有服輸的精神，而且更有超越勝敗的心胸。來競爭當然要求勝利，來比賽當然想創紀錄。但是有修養的運動家，必定要達到得失無動於中的境地。運動所重，乃在運動的精神。「勝固欣然，敗亦可喜。」正是重要的運動精神之一；否則就要變成「悻悻然」的小人了！

有風度的運動家是「言必信，行必果。」的人。運動會要舉行宣誓，義即在此。臨陣脫逃，半途而廢，都不是運動家所應有的。「任重而道遠」和「貫徹始終」的精神，應由運動家表現。所以賽跑落後，無希望得獎，還要努力跑到的人，乃是有毅力的人。

運動家的風度表現在人生上，是一個莊嚴公正、協調進取的人生。有運動家風度的人，寧可有光明的失敗，決不要不榮譽的成功！

～節錄自〈新人生觀〉～

第六課　休閒①活動的新趨勢

　　現代的人在經過緊張繁忙②的生活後，總希望以各式休閒活動來舒展③疲勞④的身心。有人是以在斗室⑤中的娛樂活動來消遣⑥，如卡拉OK、狄斯可⑦、集郵⑧、下棋⑨……。有人走出戶外⑩去欣賞⑪大自然，呼吸清淨的空氣來健身，如爬山、賞雪⑫、海釣⑬、採果⑭……。但是多半參加各種活動以後，總有一些落寞⑮的感覺——勞累⑯、混亂⑰、無聊⑱、浪費……，因此有人就意識⑲到我們是否缺少⑳一些建設性㉑及教育性的休閒活動呢？於是服務性㉒休閒活動就逐漸㉓流行起來了。

　　如何安排㉔參與有意義的服務性休閒活動呢？最重要的是先有效㉕利用休閒時間，不影響正常工作。再注意工作效率，在提升生活品質前提下注重人格發展，最後達到「自己快樂，別人受惠㉖」的目標。社會上有不少各種義務性㉗的活動，都可積極㉘參加，如醫院義工㉙、社團㉚服務、維護自然生態㉛、環保㉜勸導㉝等等。

　　在國際間，由於相互關切㉞，使各國人民獻身㉟服務社會的工作十分普遍㊱。各項國際公益㊲活動可以提升青年人的愛心，也可藉此充實知識，並能增進世界性的人際關係㊳。今日世界

· 73 ·

已成為一個「地球村㊴」，有些連續遭受天災㊵人禍㊶的地區，「飢餓㊷」摧殘㊸著無數的生命，怎麼能不伸出援手去救助呢？

因此，參與服務性休閒活動行列，不但有新的體驗㊹，而且由於大家的援助，才能使受難的生命有了新的展望㊺。

一、生詞： New Vocabulary:

1. 休ㄒㄧㄡ閒ㄒㄧㄢ xiūxián *N/AT*: leisure

2. 繁ㄈㄢ忙ㄇㄤ fánmáng

   SV/AT: to be toilsome, hasseling, vexing, overburdening

   近來我的工作很繁忙。

   Recently my work has been quite overburdening.

3. 舒ㄕㄨ展ㄓㄢ shūzhǎn

   V: to unwind; to stretch; to limber; to relax

   旅行是舒展身心的好方法。

   Traveling is a good way to relax the body and mind.

4. 疲ㄆㄧ勞ㄌㄠ pílaó

   SV/N: to be weary, exhausted; weariness, exhaustion

   下班回家後洗個熱水澡，可以消除疲勞。

   After getting off work and returning home, a hot bath can eliminate exhaustion.

5. 斗ㄉㄡ室ㄕ dǒushì *N*: a small room

6. 消ㄒㄧㄠ遣ㄑㄧㄢ xiāoqiǎn

   V/N: (*a*) to kill time; to amuse oneself

   (*b*) a diversion

週末你都是怎麼消遣的？

What are doing to amuse yourself this weekend?

7. 狄斯可 dísīkě　*N*: disco

8. 集郵 jíyóu　***VO*: to collect stamps; philately**

集郵可增加歷史、地理等方面的知識。

Collecting stamps can increase one's knowledge of history, geography, etc.

9. 下棋 xiàchí　***VO*: to play chess**

我們來下一盤棋好嗎？

Let's play a game of chess, OK?

10. 戶外 hùwài　*N/AT*: outdoors

11. 欣賞 xīnshǎng　*V*: to enjoy; to appreciate

他在欣賞這個港口的夜景。

He is enjoying the view of this harbour at night.

12. 賞雪 shǎngxuě

***VO/AT*: to enjoy a view of snow, to enjoy a snow scene**

夏天可以到高山頂上去賞雪。

In summer one can go to the peak of a high mountain to enjoy a view of the snow.

13. 海釣 hǎidiào　*N*: sea fishing

14. 採果 cǎiguǒ　***VO*: to pick fruit; fruit picking**

許多果園對外開放，只要買一張門票就可以進去自由採果。

Many fruit orchards are open to the public; one merely needs to buy a ticket and then can go in and freely pick fruit.

15. 落寞 lùomò　***SV*: to be lonely, alone, desolate**

同學們都在唱歌，他一人在一旁顯得很落寞。

As his classmates are all singing together, he, off to the side, appears very lonely.

16. 勞累 láolèi　***SV/AT*: to be rundown, overworked, tired**

今天我工作了十個小時，覺得很勞累。

I worked ten hours today and felt very rundown.

17. 混亂 hǔnluàn

***SV/AT*: to be in confusion, disorder, chaos**

這個城市的交通很混亂。

This city's traffic is really disordered.

18. 無聊 wúliáo　***SV/AT*: to be boring, silly, vapid**

暑假太長，他覺得無聊，希望快點開學。

The summer vacation is too long; he feels bored and wishes to quickly begin his studies.

19. 意識 yìshì

***V/N*: (*a*) to realize; to be aware of**

　　***(b)* consciousness**

他說了幾句話以後，大家都不理他了，他意識到自己說錯了話。

After he said a few sentences, nobody respected him, he realized that he had spoken wrongly.

20. 缺少 qūeshǎo　***V*: to lack; to be short of**

這個家庭缺少一個女主人。

This house lacks a house wife.

21. 建設性 jiànshèxìng   *AT*: **constructive; useful**

請大家提出建設性的建議。

Everybody please give constructive advice.

22. 服務性 fúwùxìng   *AT*: **to be of service**

服務性的工作須要的人力越來越多。

Service work requires more and more manpower.

23. 逐漸 zhújiàn   *A*: **gradually**

天氣逐漸冷了，外出時得加一件衣服。

The weather is gradually getting colder, when going out add a layer of clothing.

24. 安排 ānpái   *V/N*: **to plan; to arrange**

他每天把自己的時間安排得很好，一點兒都不浪費。

He arranges his time very well everyday; not even a little time is wasted.

25. 有效 yǒuxiào   *SV/AT*: **to be effective, efficient, valid**

這張車票只有今天有效，明天就不能用了。

This train ticket is valid today only, tomorrow it cannot be used.

26. 受惠 shòuhùi

VO: **to receive benefit; to be benefited**

學校美化環境，使師生都受惠。

Teachers and students all benefit from beautifying the

school environment.

27. 義務性 yìwùxìng　*AT*: **voluntary; obligatory, a duty**

自私的人不喜歡做義務性的工作。

Selfish people do not like to do voluntary work.

28. 積極 jījí

SV/A/AT: **(*a*) to be positive**

(*b*) energetic, active, vigorous

(*a*) 他對工作的態度很積極。

He has a very positive attitude towards work.

(*b*) 我們要積極爭取勝利。

We want to actively strive for victory.

29. 義工 yìgōng　*N*: **volunteer**

30. 社團 shètuán

N: **a civic organization; an association; a corporation**

31. 生態 shēngtài　*N*: **ecology, ecological system**

32. 環保 huánbǎo　*N*: **environmental protection**

33. 勸導 quàndǎo　*V*: **to advise; to exhort; to guide**

我們要勸導那些亂丟煙頭的人。

We should advise those people who sloppily throw cigarette butts around.

34. 關切 guānqiè

V/N: **(*a*) to be deeply concerned; to show concern**

(*b*) concern

父母總是關切兒女的健康。

Parents are always concerned about their children's health.

35. 獻身 xiànshēn

VO: **to devote one's life to a cause, to devote one's self to a cause**

孫中山先生獻身國民革命，一共四十年。

Doctor Sun Yat-Sen altogether devoted forty years of his life to the national revolution.

36. 普遍 pǔbiàn　　*SV/AT*: **to be universal, common, general**

會操作電腦的人很普遍。

People who can operate computers are quite universal.

37. 公益 gōngyì　　*N*: **public welfare**

38. 人際關係 rénjìguānxì　　*N*: **human relations**

39. 地球村 dìqiúcūn　　*N*: **global village, world community**

40. 天災 tiānzāi　　*N*: **natural disaster**

41. 人禍 rénhùo　　*N*: **man-made disasters or accidents**

42. 飢餓 jīè　　*N*: **hunger, starvation, famine**

43. 摧殘 cūicán

V/N: **to be victimized; to suffer; to be savaged**

經過一夜暴風雨的摧殘，花園裡的花落了。

As the result of being savaged by a rainstorm one night, the flowers in the garden have fallen.

44. 體驗 tǐyàn

V/N: (*a*) **to experience firsthand**

(*b*) **firsthand experience**

他要到鄉下種田，體驗一下農人的生活。

He wants to go to the countryside and farm to experience the life of peasants firsthand.

45. 展望 zhǎnwàng

V/N: (a) to look into the distance; to look ahead

(b) a forecast; a prospect

展望未來，一片光明。

The forecast for the future is promising.

二、成語與俗語：Proverbs and Common Sayings:

1. 自己快樂，別人受惠 zìjǐkuàilèbiérénshoùhùi

When one is happy, others benefit

幫助盲人過馬路，就是一件使「自己快樂，別人受惠」的事。

Helping blind people to cross the street is a way in which "When one is happy, others benefit".

三、句型：Sentence Patterns:

1. 由於……使……

as the result of X......Y has happened

......can......it can also help to...... finally it can......

(1) 由於他的幫助，使我找到了一個好工作。

(2) 由於他的勸告，使我戒煙了。

(3) 最近由於天天下雨，使河水漲了。

2.……可以……也可以藉此……並能

...... can...... in addition, it makes it possible to...... and simultaneously can......

because of X...Y has been the result...

(1) 運動可以使身體健康，也可藉此交朋友，並能改掉貪睡的習慣。

(2) 種花可以陶冶性情，也可藉此認識植物，並能美化環境。

(3) 各國之間的文化交流可以增進彼此的了解，也可藉此建立友誼，並能促進世界大同。

四、字音辨識：Characters with multiple pronuciations and meanings:

1. 參　(1) cān ㄘㄢ　加入。例如：參加。

　　　　　to get involved in, to participate in

　　　(2) cēn ㄘㄣ　例如：參差──不整齊的樣子。

　　　　　to be of different, varied or irregular sizes

　　　(3) sān ㄙㄢ　「三」的大寫。

　　　　　The formal form of writing the number "3" (NOTE: In Chinese there is both a formal and informal way of writing the numbers from 0 to 10. The formal style is as follows:

　　　　　零，壹，貳，參，肆，伍，陸，柒，捌，玖，拾）。

　　　(4) shēn ㄕㄣ　也叫人參。一種植物，根部大，可作藥。

　　　　　Ginseng (a Chinese herb)

2. 與　(1) yǔ ㄩˇ　和、跟、同。例如：「我與他」。

and, with, together

(2) yú ㄩˊ　同「歟」，助詞。

an interrogative particle

(3) yù ㄩˋ　參加。例如：參與。

to participate in, to take part in

3.率　(1) shùai ㄕㄨㄞˋ　帶領。例如：率領

to lead, to command

(2) lǜ ㄌㄩˋ

　　a.一定的能力。例如：效率，速率。

a limit (ie: speed limit)

a rate (ie: rate of consumption)

　　b.比例中相比的數。例如：百分率。

a ratio (in mathematics), a measure

4.重　(1) zhòng ㄓㄨㄥˋ　輕的相反詞。

heavy, weighty

(2) chúng ㄔㄨㄥˊ

　　a.複疊。例如：重複，重疊。

to pile one upon another, to layer, to superimpose

　　b.再，另。例如：重寫。

to copy, to duplicate, to repeat

5.切　(1) qīe ㄑㄧㄝ　用刀割。例如：切肉，切水果。

to cut, to slice, to carve, to mince

(2) qìe ㄑㄧㄝˋ

　　a.密合。例如：密切。

to be close to emotionally

   b. 急迫。例如：迫切。

to be urgent, to be pressing

   c. 「一切」就是全部的意思。

to be all, to be everything

五、問題討論：Problems and Discussions:

1. 參加一般性的休閒活動，有什麼感覺？

_____

2. 請寫出十種戶外活動。你認為哪一種最有趣？為什麼？

_____

3. 為什麼服務性的休閒活動會逐漸流行起來？怎麼安排參加？

_____

4. 能達到「自己快樂別人受惠」的活動有哪些？

_____

5. 為什麼今日世界已成為一個地球村？

_____

6. 參加國際性公益活動有什麼好處？為什麼？

_____

六、練習：Practice Exercises:

1. 填空：

Fill in the blanks:

例：(1)休閒活動 _____活動；_____活動。

   (2) 落寞的感覺 _____感覺；_____感覺。

(3) 建設性的活動　建設性的 _____；建設性的 ____。

(4) 利用時間 _____時間；_____時間。

(5) 影響工作　影響_____；影響_____。

(6) 提升品質　提升_____；提升_____。

(7) 社團服務 _____服務；_____服務。

(8) 環保勸導　環保_____；環保_____。

(9) 充實知識　充實_____；充實_____。

(10) 摧殘生命　摧殘_____；摧殘_____。

2. 改錯：

Correct the mistakes:

(1) 聽音樂是最好的消遺方法。_____

(2) 我不太欣常這幅名畫。_____

(3) 空氣這麼晴淨，去慢跑吧！_____

(4) 這種無柳的工作沒有人願意做。_____

(5) 績極一點總比消極好。_____

(6) 戰爭催殘了不少生命。_____

(7) 籍去外國的機會，多交一些朋友。_____

(8) 非洲有些地區常糟受天災。_____

3. 選擇：

Select the best word:

____(1) 站在海邊真能：

舒服
舒適　⎬ 平日勞累的精神。
舒展

＿＿＿(2) 大家都在跳狄斯可，她一人坐在角落，顯得十分

　　　　寂寞 ⎫
　　　　落寞 ⎬　＿＿＿＿＿＿＿＿。
　　　　冷寞 ⎭

＿＿＿(3) 他日常生活不太正常，影響了他工作的

　　　　有效 ⎫
　　　　效能 ⎬　＿＿＿＿＿＿＿＿。
　　　　效率 ⎭

＿＿＿(4) 有了安定的工作，就要想如何

　　　　提升 ⎫
　　　　提到 ⎬　＿＿＿＿＿＿＿＿生活品質。
　　　　提起 ⎭

＿＿＿(5) 參觀 ⎫
　　　　參與 ⎬　＿＿＿＿＿＿＿＿有意義的活動，可使自己
　　　　參考 ⎭　快樂別人受惠。

＿＿＿(6) 在服務社會的

　　　　題目 ⎫
　　　　問題 ⎬　＿＿＿＿＿＿＿＿下，各種義務性的活動都
　　　　前提 ⎭　可以參加。

＿＿＿(7) 由於相互

　　　　關切 ⎫
　　　　深切 ⎬　＿＿＿＿＿＿＿＿增進不少世界各國之間的
　　　　親切 ⎭　人際關係。

___(8) 環保工作包括不少主題，最重要的是

維持
維續 } ＿＿＿＿＿＿自然生態。
維護

4.造句：

Make Sentences:

(1) 欣賞：＿＿＿＿＿＿＿＿＿＿＿＿＿＿＿＿＿＿

(2) 有效：＿＿＿＿＿＿＿＿＿＿＿＿＿＿＿＿＿＿

(3) 勸導：＿＿＿＿＿＿＿＿＿＿＿＿＿＿＿＿＿＿

(4) 普遍：＿＿＿＿＿＿＿＿＿＿＿＿＿＿＿＿＿＿

(5) 充實：＿＿＿＿＿＿＿＿＿＿＿＿＿＿＿＿＿＿

第七課　單親①家庭

　　所謂「單親家庭」，是指夫妻②因離婚③、分居、死亡、遺棄④、服刑⑤等原因而造成雙親之一單獨與子女組成的家庭。

　　單親家庭不是破碎⑥家庭，更不一定會過不幸的生活，只要單親媽媽（或爸爸）面對問題，重新安排生活，家人仍能過得自在⑦而有意義。

　　離婚的婦女，除了分離的痛苦⑧（可能因此要忍痛⑨離開子女），有時還得面對社會異樣⑩的眼光⑪。喪偶⑫的妻子要承擔⑬很大的傷痛，須付出很大的心力來克服⑭。職業婦女，雖有工作能力，但因家中少一個生產人口，經濟上可能面臨⑮一些難題，有些家庭主婦因此被迫成為職業婦女而增加生活的壓力。

　　除了失去先生（或太太）的力量和意見共同教養子女以外，孩子因失去父親或母親的打擊⑯，而情緒⑰行為受到很多影響。父母親不但要付出更多的愛和支持，更要承受子女的情緒反彈⑱，因此增加許多不安。

　　單親爸爸有兩種情況，一種人忙著約會，希望新交女朋友可以分擔⑲照顧⑳孩子的責任㉑，有的人甚至把這種責任完全丟給新女友。另一種人往往害怕讓孩子受到傷害，因此除非時機㉒

成熟㉓，他不願女友出現在孩子面前。離婚的單親爸爸的錢都花在孩子身上，或許他還要付贍養費㉔，這種經濟壓力顯然㉕會促使㉖他們逃避婚姻。

　　單親家庭與其痛苦生活，不如選擇㉗接受事實，面對問題，重新安排生活。單親媽媽（或爸爸）首先應該學習處理自己的生活情緒，給自己成長的機會。要是情緒不穩，體力難負擔，最好先把孩子托給親人照顧一陣子，坦然㉘接受朋友同事精神上的支持和協助。或是找專業的輔導㉙機構，尋求適應生活的良好方法。另外，根據自己的體能、時間、個性和條件，參與適當的社會團體或學習技藝，不但增加社交機會，也開拓㉚了更寬廣㉛的空間。

　　失去父親或母親對孩子多少有些傷害，父母親應調適㉜自己，以平常心面對子女，不能因可憐孩子而過度寵愛㉝，或用物質彌補㉞。

　　單親媽媽（或爸爸）應該先學習讓自己獨立，再處理前次婚姻留下的創痛㉟，遇到適合對象，仍可再創自己的第二春㊱。

一、生詞：New Vocabulary:

1. 單ㄉㄢ親ㄑㄧㄣ　dānqīn　*N*: single parent; sole guardian

2. 夫ㄈㄨ妻ㄑㄧ　fūqī

　　N: both parents, father and mother, husband and wife

3. 離ㄌㄧ婚ㄏㄨㄣ　líhūn　*VO*: to divorce; to be divorced

　　他們已經離婚十年了，都還沒再結婚。

They have already been divorced for ten years; neither of them has as yet remarried.

4. 遺棄 yíqì

V: to abandon; to forsake; to leave uncared for

丈夫遺棄太太或太太遺棄丈夫造成的單親家庭很多。

Husbands abandoning their wives or wives abandoning their husbands creates many single parent households.

5. 服刑 fúxíng　　**VO: to serve a prison term**

他犯了罪，現在正在服刑。

He committed a crime, and now he is serving a term in prison.

6. 破碎 pòsuì　　**SV: to be (to get) broken, shattered**

破碎家庭中的孩子，常常有心理上的問題。

The children of broken homes often have psychological problems.

7. 自在 zìzài　　**SV/AT: comfortable; at ease**

人人都喜歡過自由自在的生活。

Everybody likes to lead a free, comfortable life.

8. 痛苦 tòngkǔ　　**SV: to be painful, suffering, anguished**

父母離婚了，孩子們很痛苦。

When parents are divorced, the children suffer greatly.

9. 忍痛 rěntòng

VO: very reluctantly; with great reservations

她又窮又有病，忍痛把她的畫賣了。

Being both poor and sick, she very reluctantly sold her paintings.

10. 異樣 yìyàng　*AT*: **different; unusual**

離婚後，她不在乎別人用異樣的眼光看她。

After the divorce, she did not care that other people looked upon her differently.

11. 眼光 yǎnguāng　*N*: **eye; vision**

12. 喪偶 sàngǒu

VO: **to lose a spouse, to become a widow or a widower**

喪偶的人很孤單寂寞。

People who lose a spouse are very lonely.

13. 承擔 chéngdān

V: **to undertake; to assume; to bear（a duty or task）**

傳統的家庭，賺錢養家的責任由丈夫一個人承擔。

In traditional households the responsibility for making money is assumed by the husband.

14. 克服 kèfú　*V*: **to overcome; to conquer; to surmount**

做事遇到困難時，就要想法子克服。

When one comes upon a difficulty in doing something, one then needs to think of a way to surmount it.

15. 面臨 miànlín

V/N: **to be faced with; to be confronted with; to be up against**

這個國家面臨經濟危機。

This country is faced with an economic crisis.

16. 打擊 dǎjí

V/N: **(*a*) to strike; to hit; to attack**

(*b*) a blow; an attack

一連幾件不幸的事打擊她，她快要發瘋了。

A sussession of unfortunate circumstances has been a blow to her heart (Spirit), (as a result) she is getting sick.

17. 情緒 qíngxù　　**N: mood; morale; spirit**

18. 反彈 fǎntán　　**V: to respond; to strike back**

你罵別人，別人一定會反彈。

If you curse other people, other people definitely will respond.

19. 分擔 fēndān　　**V: to split responsibility; to share a burden**

養育孩子的工作應由父母二人分擔。

The rearing of children is a task which should be shared by both parents.

20. 照顧 zhàogù　　**V: to care for; to look after; to attend to**

夫妻都上班，小孩一定要請人照顧。

If both the husband and wife work, then they must ask others to look after the small children.

21. 責任 zérèn　　**N: a responsibility; a duty**

22. 時機 shíjī

N: an opportunity; a chance; an opportune moment

23. 成熟 chéngshú　　**SV: to ripen, mature**

不成熟的水果多半是酸的。

Most unripened fruits are sour.

24. 贍養費 shànyǎngfèi

   N: alimony, money payed to a divorced spouse (often for child support)

25. 顯然 xiǎnrán　　*A*: obviously; evidently

她今天不理我，顯然是生我的氣。

She is discourteous to me today, evidently she has become angry with me.

26. 促使 cùshǐ　　*V*: to encourage; to impel; to spur on

愛美的心促使她減肥。

Her love of beauty impelled her to lose weight.

27. 選擇 xuǎnzé

   V/N: (*a*) to make a choice; to select

   　　(*b*) a selection; a choice

選擇一個好伴侶是很重要的事。

Choosing a good companion is a very important business.

28. 坦然 tǎnrán　　*SV/A*: to calmly do something

他承認自己做錯了事，坦然地接受處罰。

He acknowledges that he did something wrongly and calmly accepts the punishment.

29. 輔導 fǔdǎu　　*V*: to coach; to tutor

放學後，老師輔導一些成績比較差的學生。

After school the teacher tutors some underachieving students.

30. 開拓 kāituò　*V*: to open up; to expand

多看書，可以開拓我們的知識。

Reading more books can expand our knowledge.

31. 寬廣 kuānguǎng　*SV*: to be vast, broad, extensive

這個運動場很寬廣。

This exercise field is quite vast.

32. 調適 tiáoshì

V: to prepare; to brace; to collect; to adjust; to adapt

受到打擊之後，要好好調適自己。

After sustaining a blow one should brace one's self.

33. 寵愛 chǒngài　*V*: to dote on; to make a pet of somebody

對孩子不可太寵愛。

You should not dote on children too much.

34. 彌補 míbǔ

V: to remedy; to make good; to make up (after a fight); to make retribution

做錯了事、說錯了話，都要想法子彌補。

Doing something wrongly or saying something wrongly both require one to think of a way make retribution.

35. 創痛 chuāngtòng

N: an emotional hurt, an emotional wound

36. 第二春 dièrchūn

N: a second spring; a rebirth; a second chance

二、句型：Sentence Patterns:

1. 所謂……是指……

the so called......is meant to mean......;

this so called......is supposed to signify......;

By saying......we mean to say...... \

(1) 所謂超市是指超級市場。

(2) 所謂單身貴族是指沒結婚、收入不錯的人。

(3) 所謂第二春是指第二次結婚。

2. 不是……更不一定……

is not...... and it really is not certain that......;

(1) 他不是美國人，更不一定是英國人。

(2) 結婚不是愛情的墳墓，更不一定會過不好的生活。

(3) 她不是討厭你，更不一定不願跟你做朋友。

3. 只要……仍能……

only needs to......still can.......;

only requires that......then still can be able to......

(1) 妳只要努力，仍能趕上同學。

(2) 只要每天運動，雖然年紀大了，仍能保持身體的健康。

(3) 只要改掉壞習慣，仍能過正常的生活。

4. 與其……不如……

doing X......is not as good as doing Y......;

After weighing the pros and cons, X is not as good a decision as Y

(1) 與其看電影不如爬山。

Marvel Ba

091 6610 899

(2) 與其吃西餐不如吃中餐。

(3) 與其過孤獨的生活不如多交朋友。

5. 要是……最好先……

If......it would be best to first......

(1) 要是她不理你,你最好先向她道歉。

(2) 你要是向她求婚,最好先送她一束玫瑰花。

(3) 你要是想學書法,最好先買一枝好毛筆。

三、字音辨識：Characters with multiple pronuciations and meanings:

1. 喪　(1) sāng ㄙㄤ　埋葬死人的事。例如：喪事。

of death, funeral; to mourn

(2) sàng ㄙㄤ丶　失去。例如：喪失。

to be deprived of, to lose

2. 彈　(1) tán ㄊㄢˊ　用手指撥弄或敲打。例如：彈琴。

to pluck, to beat, to tap

(2) dàn ㄉㄢ丶　槍、砲等用的鐵丸。例如：子彈、砲
彈。

a pellet, a bullet

3. 擔　(1) dān ㄉㄢ　負責。例如：擔任、承擔。用肩挑。例
如：擔水。

to take upon oneself, to shoulder, to bear

(2) dàn ㄉㄢ丶　挑子。例如：擔子、重擔。

a load, a burden

4. 調　(1) tiáo ㄊㄧㄠˊ　和合。例如：調和、調適。

to mix, to blend, to harmonize

(2) diào ㄉㄧㄠˋ　音樂的聲律。例如：曲調。

a tune, a melody

5.創　　(1) chuāng ㄔㄨㄤ　傷。例如：創口、創痛。

a wound

(2) chuàng ㄔㄨㄤˋ　開始。例如：創造。

to begin, to initiate, to start, to create

四、問題討論：Questions for Discussion:

1. 造成單親家庭的原因只有死亡及離婚嗎？還有沒有別的原因？

_____

2. 父母在家庭中時常吵架對孩子有什麼直接的影響？

_____

3. 父母離婚後，對孩子造成什麼心理不平衡的陰影？

_____

4. 「單親孩童」在校的成績受家庭影響嗎？為什麼？

_____

5. 為什麼「單親孩童」不喜歡別人的同情和憐憫？

_____

五、練習：Practice Exercises:

1. 選擇相反詞：

Select the word with the opposite meaning:

⑴ 服刑：____　　*a.*旅行　*b.*坐牢　*c.*出獄

⑵ 破碎：____　　*a.*完整　*b.*一半　*c.*弄壞

　　(3) 面對：＿＿　　　　*a.*反對　　*b.*面臨　　*c.*逃避

　　(4) 忍痛：＿＿　　　　*a.*被迫　　*b.*樂意　　*c.*忍耐

　　(5) 克服：＿＿　　　　*a.*屈服　　*b.*戰勝　　*c.*困難

　　(6) 被迫：＿＿　　　　*a.*被逼　　*b.*自由　　*c.*自願

　　(7) 支持：＿＿　　　　*a.*依靠　　*b.*打擊　　*c.*幫助

　　(8) 事實：＿＿　　　　*a.*幻想　　*b.*實在　　*c.*想法

　　(9) 穩：＿＿　　　　　*a.*動搖　　*b.*安定　　*c.*隱藏

　　⑩ 過度：＿＿　　　　*a.*過分　　*b.*正當　　*c.*適當

2.選擇相似詞：

Select the word with a similar meaning:

　　(1) 不幸：　＿＿　　　*a.*倒楣　　*b.*幸運　　*c.*辛苦

　　(2) 自在：　＿＿　　　*a.*自由　　*b.*隨時　　*c.*美妙

　　(3) 承擔：　＿＿　　　*a.*重擔　　*b.*分享　　*c.*負擔

　　(4) 專業：　＿＿　　　*a.*專心　　*b.*專門　　*c.*專家

　　(5) 處理：　＿＿　　　*a.*辦理　　*b.*整理　　*c.*修理

　　(6) 一陣子：＿＿　　　*a.*一陣風　*b.*短時間　*c.*長時間

　　(7) 根據：　＿＿　　　*a.*證據　　*b.*按照　　*c.*依法

　　(8) 開拓：　＿＿　　　*a.*開始　　*b.*拓展　　*c.*拓荒

　　(9) 彌補：　＿＿　　　*a.*補習　　*b.*補洞　　*c.*補救

　　⑩ 適宜：　＿＿　　　*a.*合適　　*b.*舒適　　*c.*適應

3.造句：

Make Sentences:

　　(1) 遺棄＿＿＿＿＿＿＿＿＿＿＿＿＿＿＿＿＿＿＿＿＿＿＿＿

　　(2) 破碎＿＿＿＿＿＿＿＿＿＿＿＿＿＿＿＿＿＿＿＿＿＿＿＿

　　(3) 異樣＿＿＿＿＿＿＿＿＿＿＿＿＿＿＿＿＿＿＿＿＿＿＿＿

(4) 克服 _____

(5) 照顧 _____

(6) 坦然 _____

(7) 成熟 _____

(8) 分擔 _____

(9) 寵愛 _____

(10) 促使 _____

閱讀與探討
Read and Discuss

單親家庭

劇中人
張太太（太）張美英的母親 王老師（師）張美英的國中二年級導師

（按電鈴聲）

師：張太太，您好。我是美英的國中導師，現在能不能跟你談談？

太：歡迎，歡迎！請進，請進！

師：美英是一個早熟懂事的孩子。她把最近家庭變動的情形，不但告訴了班上幾位要好的同學，同時也寫在週記上讓我知道。因為你要上班，所以她多分擔點家務，照顧弟妹，身心有時覺得疲累，因此成績退步了一些。

太：謝謝你對美英的關心。沒想到美英這麼大方地把家裡的事告訴同學。不像她念國小的弟妹，都不願向外透露，免得同學會嘲笑他們。美英到底是大孩子了，以往她爸爸一回家就跟我吵，這樣真

是影響了孩子，也對不起孩子，這也是我再三考慮跟她父親離婚的原因。給孩子一個清靜的環境，好讓他們能專心地做功課，正常地生活。

師：我在她的週記中發現她因為母親常指責父親的不是，而使她更加同情母親，責怪父親。我想這樣不好吧！很容易造成孩子心裡不平衡的陰影。建議你應當告訴孩子每個家庭有不同的婚姻模式，父母的例子，不能代表所有兩性的關係，給孩子們建立一個正確的觀念。

太：謝謝你的好建議，我以後會多留意。至於我的上班，也是不得已的，否則如何維持家庭生活？她父親一走了之，就什麼都不管了。這樣的生活剛開始，我跟孩子都不習慣，等過一陣子適應過來就會好些。

師：聽到你這樣說，我很高興也放心多了。

太：謝謝你發現問題，及早來做家庭訪問，給我們一些提醒和指導。今後還盼多多指教。

師：指教不敢當，我們常常保持聯絡，多溝通就好了。時間不早了，我得向你告辭了。再見！

太：有空歡迎常來。再見！

問答：Answer the following questions:

1. 你認為男孩比較早熟，還是女孩比較早熟？

_____

2. 學生為什麼不喜歡導師到家裡去做家庭訪問？

_____

3. 美英是國中二年級學生，她大概十幾歲？她在家都能幫母親做些什

麼？

_____

4. 美英為什麼成績日漸退步？

_____

5. 美英國小的弟妹為什麼不願向同學透露家裡的事？

_____

6. 美英母親說因為什麼原因才要跟美英爸爸離婚？

_____

7. 家裡沒有清靜的環境，對孩子有什麼影響？

_____

8. 老師說美英心理不平衡的陰影是什麼？老師的好建議是什麼？

_____

9. 你認為美英的父親是一個負責的人嗎？為什麼？

_____

10. 你想美英老師做過家庭訪問後，她母親會注意美英生活上哪些問題？

_____

佳文欣賞

我的母親

胡　適

　　我母親二十三歲做了寡婦，又是當家的後母。這種生活的痛苦，我的笨筆寫不出一萬分之一二。家中財政本不寬裕，全靠二哥在上海經營調度。大哥從小就是敗子，吸鴉片、賭博，

錢到手就光，光了就回家打主意，見了香爐就拿出去賣，撈著錫茶壺就拿出去押。我母親幾次邀了本家長輩來，給他定下每月用費的總目。但他總不夠用，到處都欠下了煙債、賭債。每年除夕，我家中總有一大群討債的，每人一盞燈籠，坐在大廳上不肯去。大哥早已避出去了。大廳的兩排椅子上，滿滿的都是燈籠和債主。我母親走進走出，料理年夜飯、謝灶神、壓歲錢等事，只當做不曾看見這一群人。到了近半夜，快要「封門」了，我母親才走後門出去，央一位鄰舍本家到我家來，每一家債戶開發一點錢。做好做歹的，這一群討債的才一個一個提著燈籠走出去。一會兒，大哥敲門回來了。我母親從不罵他一句。並且因為是新年，她臉上從不露出一點怒色。這樣的過年，我過了六七次。

大嫂是個最無能而又最不懂事的人，二嫂是個很能幹而氣量很窄小的人。她們常常鬧意見，只因為我母親的和氣榜樣，她們還不曾有公然相罵相打的事。她們鬧氣時，只是不說話，不答話，把臉放下來，叫人難看；二嫂生氣時臉色變青，更是怕人。她們對我母親鬧氣時也是如此。我起初全不懂得這一套，後來也漸漸懂得看人的臉色了。我漸漸明白，世間最可厭惡的事，莫如一張生氣的臉；世間最下流的事，莫如把生氣的臉擺給旁人看。這比打罵還難受。

我母親的氣量大，性子好，又因為做了後母後婆，她更事事留心，事事格外容忍。大哥的女兒比我小一歲，她的飲食衣

料總是和我的一樣。我和她有小爭執，總是我吃虧，母親總是責備我，要我事事讓她。後來大嫂二嫂都生了兒子了，她們生氣時便打罵孩子來出氣，一面打，一面用尖刻有刺的話罵給別人聽。我母親只裝做不聽見。有時候，她實在忍不住了，便悄悄走出門去，或到左鄰立大嬸家去坐一會，或走後門到後鄰度嫂家去閒談。她從不和兩個嫂子吵一句嘴。

第八課　青壯年的生活觀①

　　大學畢業以前是極重要的人格養成階段，畢業後各奔前程，正是人格發展的開始——擁有②不同個性、特質③的男女，藉由工作、深造④、擇偶⑤、結婚、生子、創業，開始人生的旅途。二十五歲是年輕人踏入社會的起點，直到四十歲，這就是俗稱的青壯年時期。一般人找到第一份工作，完成終身大事，初為人父母，都在這階段發生，所以稱為生命的黃金時段。不同的年紀，各有其所操心⑥的事務，而背後也多少隱藏⑦了一些問題和危機⑧。

　　青壯年在結婚和不結婚之間，最容易顯明的危機是挑剔⑨對象、單身貴族和七年之癢。其實單身者不妨⑩告訴他人我未婚，這樣給自己機會也給別人機會。因為結婚會促成男女雙方個性的改變，這種修正⑪有助於婚姻的和諧和美滿⑫。

　　俗話說：「男怕入錯行」，男性在選擇職業、投入工作上，比女性遭遇⑬更多的困擾⑭，易產生跳槽⑮、成就感⑯和信心的危機。如果男性能明白知足常樂，又能力行⑰、忍耐⑱，就不會隨意跳槽失去信心，而累積⑲的經驗會不斷地⑳增強信心，可以說用時間來換取一切。另外，多看親職教育的書，多花時間

與子女相處，除專業以外，應該保持活潑的心思去探觸㉑其他的領域㉒。女性則不要以家庭主婦的身分畫地自限，拋棄㉓婚前的工作和人際關係。婆媳㉔雙方如能誠意溝通，就可以改善彼此之間的關係。一個人能不事事求完美，就可以過得更快樂一點。

　　經濟方面，從男女雙方各有固定㉕的收入、經濟獨立，到婚後自組小家庭、生兒育女、現實生活的各項開支，使得薪水階級飽受㉖無住屋之苦（無殼危機）和錢幣貶值㉗的危機。若能當用則用，當省則省，懂得量入為出，多少能有一點儲蓄㉘，以備不時之須或是做購屋的計畫。

　　因此不論問題大小，危機或隱或顯，都應看成人生歷程中重要的思考點㉙，才能有助於人生的開展。

一、生詞：New Vocabulary:

1. 生活觀 shēnghúoguān

   N: attitude towards life; lifestyle

2. 擁有 yǒngyǒu　**V: to possess; to have; to own**

   他擁有三家公司，是個成功的商人。

   He owns three companies and is a successful businessman.

3. 特質 tèzhí

   N: characteristics; peculiarities; special qualities

4. 深造 shēnzào

   V: to take advanced level training; to take an advanced course of study

他大學畢業後進研究所深造。

After graduating from university he entered graduate school for advanced level training.

5. 擇偶 zéǒu *VO*: **to select a spouse, to select a mate**

如何擇偶是青年男女關心的問題。

How to select a spouse is a question of concern to young men and women.

6. 操心 cāoxīn *VO*: **to feel concern; to worry about**

父母總是為他們的子女操心。

Parents are always worried about their children.

7. 隱藏 yǐncáng *V*: **to hide; to conceal**

聰明的人常常隱藏他的聰明。

Smart people often conceal their intelligence.

8. 危機 wéijī *N*: **a crisis**

9. 挑剔 tiāoti

V: **to nitpick, to find fault with somebody or something**

那對夫妻總是互相挑剔，可能會離婚。

That husband and wife are always finding fault with each other; they might get divorced.

10. 不妨 bùfáng *A*: **might as well; there is no harm in**

要想了解每課書的內容，不妨多查字典。

If you want to understand the content of every lesson, you might as well look more things up in the dictionary.

11. 修正 xīuzhèng *V*: **to revise; to ammend**

你對金錢的看法必須修正一下。金錢不一定是萬能的。

You should revise your views on money. Money is not necessarily all powerful.

12. 美滿 měimǎn

SV/AT: to be perfectly satisfactory, happy, sweet

美滿的婚姻靠互愛、互信。

A happy marriage depends on mutual love and mutual trust.

13. 遭遇 zāoyù　**N: bitter experience; a hard lot**

14. 困擾 kùnrǎo

V/N: (a) to trouble; to harass; to worry

　　　　(b) a trouble; a worry; a puzzle

工作上的問題困擾了他很久。

Problems at work troubled him for a long time.

15. 跳槽 tiàocáo

VO: to get a new job, to abandon one occupation in favor of another

你常常跳槽，別人會覺得你不可靠。

You often switch jobs; others may feel that you are unreliable.

16. 成就感 chéngjiùgǎn

N: feeling of accomplishment; feeling of success

17. 力行 lìxíng

V: to practice energetically; to perform energetically; to

act with might

我們要力行我們認為對的事。

We want to practice energetically those things we believe to be right.

18. 忍耐 rěnnài

V/N: (a) to exercise patience; to be patient; to exercise sel-frestraint

(b) patience; self-restraint

那家商店的店員態度太壞，他忍耐不住，跟她吵起來了。

The clerk at that store has a bad attitude; he impatiently shouted at her.

19. 累積 lěijī

V/N: (a) to accumulate

(b) an accumulation

一個人累積多年來的經驗是很寶貴的。

The experience a person accumulates over many years is very valuable.

20. 不斷地 búduànde

AT: unceasingly; continuously; constantly; uninterruptedly

不論學什麼，都要不斷地努力，才能學好。

No matter what one studies one must unceasingly exert one's abilities in order to study well.

21. 探觸 tànchù

V: to work one's way through; to work out; to explore

這門學問我還沒探觸過，所以完全不懂。

I still have not explored this school of thought, so I completely don't understand this.

22. 領域 lǐngyù

   N: a territory; a domain; a sphere; a realm; a field

23. 拋棄 pāoqì　　*V*: to discard; to forsake; to desert

   拋棄家庭的人，將來一定會後悔的。

   People who desert their homes definitely will regret it in the future.

24. 婆媳 póxí

   N: mother-in-law and daughter-in-law (a woman and her son's wife)

25. 固定 gùdìng　　*SV/AT*: to fix, regularize, stabilize

   他沒有固定的工作，所以生活不安定。

   He does not have fixed work, so his life is not settled.

26. 飽受 bǎoshòu

   V: to suffer (an insult, a grievance, an experience) to the fullest extent

   上下班時，大家飽受塞車之苦。

   When going to or returning from work everybody suffers the misery of traffic jams.

27. 貶值 biǎnzhí

   VO: (of currency) to depreciate; to devaluate; devaluation; depreciation

美元貶值了，日圓升值了。

The American dollar has depreciated in value, the Japanese yen has appreciated in value.

28. 儲蓄 chúxù

V/N: (*a*) **to save; to deposit**

(*b*) **savings; a deposit**

從小就養成儲蓄的習慣是很好的。

It is a good thing to cultivate from childhood the habit of saving.

29. 思考點 sīkǎodiǎn

N: **a consideration; an issue to be pondered; something to be contemplated**

二、成語與俗語：Proverbs and Common Sayings:

1. 各奔前程 gèbēnqiánchéng

Each pursues his own distinct goal (without caring about others' affairs); every man for himself

大學畢業後，大家各奔前程，很難見面了。

After graduating from University everybody pursued their own goals; it is very hard to meet with them.

2. 終身大事 zhōngshēndàshì

A great event affecting one's whole life (especially referring to marriage); A turning-point in one's life

結婚是一個人的終身大事。

Marriage is a great turning-point in one's life.

3. 黃金時段 húangjīnshíduàn

prime time; the best time, the best period of time

每晚八點鐘是電視的黃金時段。

Eight o'clock every evening is television's prime time.

4. 單身貴族 dānshēngùizú

(literally: "unmarried aristocracy"), A well-paid bachelor or bachelorete, an unmarried man or woman with a highpaying job

收入多，可是沒結婚的人叫做單身貴族。

Unmarried people with large salaries are said to be "unmarried aristocracy".

5. 男怕入錯行 nánpàrùcùoháng

Men fear entering the wrong profession, Men fear getting into the wrong line of business.

「男怕入錯行」就是男人怕做一種不適合他或不好的工作。

"Man fear entering the wrong trade" means that men are afraid of doing work which is unsuitable or not good for them.

6. 知足常樂 zhīzúchánglè

Contentment brings happiness; to find happiness by being content with what one has; to be content (and therefore happy) with one's lot in life

知足常樂的人從來不發牢騷。

Those who are content with their lot in life never complain.

7. 畫地自限 huàdìzìxiàn

to try to limit oneself; to impose restrictions on oneself

一直向前走吧，不要畫地自限。

Always keep moving forward, one never wants to limit oneself.

8. 量入為出 liàngrùwéichū

to regulate expenses according to income, to limit one's expenses

量入為出的人不必向別人借錢。

People who are trying to limit their expenses must not borrow money from others.

9. 以備不時之須 yǐbèibùshízhīxū

to prepare for the unexpected (with money), to save against any eventuality

我們每個月都要儲蓄一點錢，以備不時之須。

Every month we like to save a little money, to prepare for the unexpected.

10. 或隱或顯 hùoyǐnhùoxiǎn

to sometimes be hidden and sometimes be apparent; to sporadically appear

你的病或隱或顯，一定要去醫院檢查。

Your disease appears sporadically, you should definitely go to the hospital and get examined.

三、句型： Sentence Patterns:

1. 藉由……開始……

......by means of......was able to begin...... ;

......by relying on......began to...... ;

......on the strength of......got a chance to begin......

(1) 他藉由朋友的介紹，開始工作。

(2) 王先生藉由家人的幫助，開始創業。

(3) 她藉由老師的引導，開始畫油畫。

2. 如果……又……就不會

If......as well as......then there is no way that...... ;

If......and in addition......then it is not possible that......

(1) 如果你能戒煙，又不喝酒，你的太太就不會生氣了。

(2) 如果你每天來上課，又很用功地溫習，就不會考不及格了。

(3) 他如果早一點起來，走路又快一點，就不會遲到了。

四、字音辨識： Characters with multiple pronunciations and meanings:

1. 稱　　(1) chēng ㄔㄥ

　　a. 叫。例如：我們稱他為大哥。

　　　to call (by a certain name)

　　b. 用秤量輕重。例如：稱稱看有多重。

　　　to weigh, to measure weight

　　c. 讚美。例如：稱讚。

　　　to praise, to acclaim

(2) chèng ㄔㄥˋ

　　a. 同秤。量輕重之物。

　　　a balance scale or steelyard scale（for determi-

　　　ning weight）

　　b. 適合。例如：稱職。

　　　suitable, fit, proper

(3) chèn ㄔㄣˋ　合意。例如：稱心如意。

　　in accord with, fit, suitable

2.背　　(1) bēi ㄅㄟ　負荷。例如：背著書包，背小孩。

　　　to bear（a load, burden, etc.）, to carry on the back

(2) bèi ㄅㄟˋ

　　a. 胸的後面。例如：背部。

　　　behind, the back, the reverse side, the back side

　　b. 違反，例如：違背。

　　　to rebel, to go against, to violate, to run counter to

3.處　　(1) chǔ ㄔㄨˇ

　　a. 共同工作或生活。例如：她們婆媳之間處得

　　　很好。

　　　to get along well together, to work well together

　　b. 辦理。例如：處理。

　　　to manage, to handle, to deal with, to dispose of

(2) chù ㄔㄨˋ　地方。例如：處所。

　　a location, a place, a spot, a locality

4.應　　(1) yīng ㄧㄥ　該當。例如：應該。

should, ought to

(2) yìng ㄧㄥˋ

    a. 對答。例如：應付。

    to cope with, to deal with

    b. 允許。例如：答應。

    to assent to, to permit, to allow

5. 分　　(1) fēn ㄈㄣ

    a. 離開。例如：分離。

    to divide, to distinguish, to part, to distribute, to share

    b. 一小時的 1/60。例如：一分鐘。

    one minute

(2) fèn ㄈㄣˋ　各自所佔的範圍。例如：職分、名分。

a role or part (played by a person in life), what is within a person's scope of rights, duties or obligations

6. 累　　(1) lěi ㄌㄟˇ　積聚。例如：累積。

to accumulate over a length of time, to gather up through a period of time, to pile up over time

(2) lèi ㄌㄟˋ　疲勞。例如：太累了。

to be tired, to be worn out, to be weary, to be exhausted

(3) léi ㄌㄟˊ　拖累、麻煩。例如：累贅。

a nuisance, a troublesome thing, a burden

五、問題討論：Questions and Discussions:

1. 為什麼二十五歲到四十歲是一個人的黃金時段？

_____

2. 你認為單身貴族的生活怎麼樣？

_____

3. 你認為一個家庭有幾個子女最好？

_____

4. 事事求完美的人快樂嗎？為什麼？

_____

5. 青壯年時期的男人和女人應該注意什麼？

_____

6. 你對七年之癢有什麼看法？

_____

六、練習：Practice Exercises:

1. 選擇：

Select the correct meaning:

(1) 擇　　偶＿＿　　a.選好的數字

　　　　　　　　　b.選好的職業

　　　　　　　　　c.選好的先生或太太

(2) 創　　業＿＿　　a.在別人公司幫忙

　　　　　　　　　b.正在找工作

　　　　　　　　　c.開創事業

(3) 七年之癢＿＿　　a.身體有七年的皮膚病

b.夫妻結婚一段時期，有換口味的感覺

c.夫妻結婚七年後，要創新事業

(4) 單身貴族＿＿＿　　a.不論男女他的祖先是皇室

b.夫妻之一是貴族

c.不結婚而有高收入的男人或女人

(5) 跳　　槽＿＿＿　　a.不滿意目前的工作，換個新工作

b.是一種跳舞方式

c.跳到水槽裡

(6) 人際關係＿＿＿　　a.跟朋友的關係不好

b.人與人之間的來往

c.跟人有親屬關係

(7) 無　殼　族＿＿＿　　a.沒有工作的人

b.沒有朋友的人

c.沒有房子住的人

(8) 錢幣貶值＿＿＿　　a.錢幣越來越能買更多的東西

b.錢幣越來越不能買更多的東西

c.錢幣一直能買一樣多的東西

(9)終身大事＿＿＿　　a.人臨死時的情形

b.也就是婚姻

c.形容一個人事業有成就

⑽量入為出＿＿＿　　a.收入不多，支出卻很多

b.收入不少，支出也不少

c.有多少收入，才支出多少

2.改錯：

Correct the mistakes:

(1) 背後也穩藏了一些危機。＿＿＿＿＿

(2) 二十五歲是年青人踏入社會的起點。＿＿＿＿＿

(3) 女姓不要以家庭主婦的身分書地自限。＿＿＿＿＿

(4) 這種休正有助於和皆美滿。＿＿＿＿＿

(5) 應保特活潑的心恩，去探獨其他的領域。＿＿＿＿＿

3.造句：

Make Sentences:

(1) 操心：＿＿＿＿＿＿＿＿＿＿＿＿＿＿＿＿＿＿

(2) 忍耐：＿＿＿＿＿＿＿＿＿＿＿＿＿＿＿＿＿＿

(3) 累積：＿＿＿＿＿＿＿＿＿＿＿＿＿＿＿＿＿＿

(4) 拋棄：＿＿＿＿＿＿＿＿＿＿＿＿＿＿＿＿＿＿

(5) 儲蓄：＿＿＿＿＿＿＿＿＿＿＿＿＿＿＿＿＿＿

閱讀與探討
Read and Discuss

同學會

劇中人

> 張成家（張）：男，三十多歲，銀行高級主管
>
> 李旦生（李）：男，三十多歲，電腦公司總經裡
>
> 王美君（王）：女，三十多歲，會計師兼家庭主婦

（大學同班同學，畢業十年後在同學會上重逢）

張：喂！老李，美君，你們也來了！

李：（同時）咳！不容易，不容易，我們十年沒見了。你們都沒變呀！

王：哎喲！你是張成家，你是李旦生沒說錯吧！

張：大家變是沒變，不過似乎加了碼，都胖了不少。

李：人到中年體態豐盈嘛！說什麼也苗條不了啦！在辦公室坐一天，再在汽車上坐幾小時，天天應酬吃喝，根本沒有運動嘛！我現在孤家寡人一個，一個人吃飽，全家都飽了。不必煩心什麼，只是有點閒散寂寞而已。怎麼不胖呢！

王：那你真是快樂神仙，好羨慕你呀！我每天都忙死了，家事做不完，先生也不管。上有老，下有小，都得我照顧。會計師事務所的事又一大堆，做不完帶回家，還得開夜車趕工，你們說苦不苦！有時還跟七十多歲的婆婆嘔氣。

李：你做不完的賬，我去幫你。

王：算了吧！大總經理！你哪裡還有工夫幫我，有時間去追追女朋友吧！

張：老李，說真的，你也該成家了。創業了那麼多年，公司有那麼好的成績，也該找個賢內助。啊！你也別挑剔得太厲害了，哪有十全十美的人呀！

李：我不挑，我從來沒挑過。只是看看我家哥哥嫂嫂姐姐姐夫他們過的那種日子，唉！真不想跳進結婚這圈套中。我現在多自由自在！

張：你這麼沒有勇氣。你看我背著一大家人，生活費、教育費、交際費再加上醫藥費，我用一塊錢的時候都得算算呢！還好我太太是個精打細算的人，家中一切由她主持，孩子知道用功，也不亂花錢。妻賢子孝，雖不十分富裕，可是也過得快樂舒服呢！

王：你命好，太太會持家，你忙工作無後顧之憂，怪不得你升為高級主管呢！可是我要為張大嫂打抱不平，她整天埋在家裡作牛作馬，她簡直是畫地自限，把自己完全關在家裡了，跟外界都沒有接觸，這人生還有什麼意思呢！

李：對呀！如果我結婚，我不會這麼對待心愛的人。我怕女人為我受罪，所以我不結婚。哈哈！

張：你別找理由啦！還是趕快找對象結婚吧！你們看，那不是陳兆高嗎？聽說他最近又換工作了。

王：我知道他本來教書呀！現在做什麼事？

張：噢！教書那是好幾年前的事了，後來我知道他跟校長搞得不好，一氣就辭了教職，去當廣播員了。

李：不是廣播員，好像做一位要人的秘書。

張：對，那又是後來的第三個工作，每個工作都做不到一年，有時還閒著沒工作。現在也不知道做什麼事了？常說「男怕入錯行」，他簡直不知道該入哪一行？

王：怪不得他整天跳槽呢！他過來了，你們跟他聊聊，我去那邊找女同學聊一下。看看她們婚後生活怎麼樣？老張，祝你永享天倫之樂，你呢！「有情人速成眷屬」！

張：希望你越忙越年輕。

李：是啊！青春永駐。

問答：Answer the following questions:

1. 為什麼人到中年會發胖？

_____

2. 你認為王美君的生活有意思嗎？這麼忙是快樂是不快樂？

_____

3. 李旦生受了什麼影響對結婚那麼怕？

_____

4. 張成家的生活算是美滿嗎？為什麼？

5. 張成家的太太完全獻身家庭，你認為該怎麼改善她的生活？

6. 像陳兆高這樣常常換工作，是好主意嗎？為什麼？

佳文欣賞

最苦與最樂

梁啟超

　　人生什麼事最苦呢？貧嗎？不是。失意嗎？不是。老嗎？死嗎？都不是。我說人生最苦的事，莫若身上背著一種未了的責任。人若能知足，雖貧不苦；若能安分（不多作分外希望），雖失意不苦；老、死乃人生難免的事，達觀的人看得很平常，也不算什麼苦。獨是凡人生在世間一天，便有應該做的事。該做的事沒有做完，便像是有幾千斤重擔子壓在肩頭，再苦是沒有的了。為什麼呢？因為受那良心責備不過，要逃躲也沒處逃躲呀！

　　答應人做一事沒有辦，欠了人家的錢沒有還，受了人家的恩惠沒有報答，得罪了人沒有賠禮，這就連這個人的面也幾乎不敢見他；縱然不見他的面，睡在夢裡，都像有他的影子來纏著我。為什麼呢？因為覺得對不住他呀！因為自己對他的責任，還沒有解除呀！不獨是對於一個人如此，就是對於家庭、

對於社會、對於國家，乃至對於自己，都是如此。凡屬我受過他好處的人，我對於他便有了責任。凡屬我應該做的事，而且力量能夠做得到的，我對於這件事便有了責任。凡屬我自己打主意要做一件事，便是現在的自己和將來的自己立了一種契約，便是自己對於自己加一層責任。有了這責任，那良心便時時刻刻監督在後頭。一日應盡的責任沒有盡，到夜裡頭便是過著苦痛日子；一生應盡的責任沒有盡，便死也帶著苦痛往墳墓裡去。這種苦痛卻比不得普通的貧困老死，可以達觀排解得來。所以我說人生沒有苦痛便罷；若有苦痛，當然沒有比這個加重的了。

　　翻過來看，什麼事最快樂呢？自然責任完了，算是人生第一件樂事。古語說得好：「如釋重負」；俗語亦說是：「心上一塊石頭落了地」。人到這個時候，那種輕鬆愉快，真是不可以言語形容。責任越重大，負責的日子越久長，到責任完了時，海闊天空，心安理得，那快樂還要加幾倍哩！大抵天下事從苦中得來的樂才算真樂。人生須知道有負責任的苦處，才能知道有盡責任的樂處。這種苦樂循環，便是這有活力的人間一種趣味。卻是不盡責任，受良心責備，這些苦都是自己找來的。一翻過來，處處盡責任，便處處快樂；時時盡責任，便時時快樂。快樂之權，操之在己。孔子所以說：「無入而不自得。」正是這種作用。

　　有人說：「既然這苦是從負責任而生的，我若是將責任卸

卻，豈不是就永遠沒有苦了嗎？」這卻不然，責任是要解除了才沒有，並不是卸了就沒有。人生若能永遠像兩三歲小孩，本來沒有責任，那就本來沒有苦。到了長成，責任自然壓在你的肩頭上，如何能逃躲？不過有大小的分別罷了。盡得大的責任，就得大快樂；盡得小的責任，就得小快樂。你若是要逃躲，反而是自投苦海，永遠不能解除了。

《飲冰室文集》

第九課　人人都是環保尖兵

　　地球不再美麗了。你、我、他都有責任。人人都是罪魁禍首。可是我們大家都還不清醒①，都還不認錯②，仍然一天一天不斷地在刻意③破壞我們唯一生存的地方——地球。

　　清澈④揚波⑤的海洋因垃圾的污染變得死氣沉沉；青翠⑥茂密⑦的森林⑧因被濫伐⑨漸漸變成乾枯⑩的荒山⑪；寬廣清幽⑫的原野⑬因工廠的濃煙⑭與廢氣⑮變得烏煙瘴氣；山邊潺潺⑯的溪流⑰也因污水及化學廢水的流入成為混濁⑱帶色的臭溝⑲。……這樣下去，地球還能美麗嗎？要知道我們只有一個地球啊！人類把這個僅有的，獨一無二的美麗家園破壞到目前這種慘不忍睹的程度，怎不令人惋惜！

　　日趨嚴重的情況不只是在地球表面上，甚至在地球上空保護我們的臭氧層⑳都成了百孔千瘡的破網㉑，太陽最有威力的紫外線㉒現在都能直接傷害到我們嬌嫩㉓的皮膚㉔了。

　　早在二十年前透過全球數千名環保志士的登高一呼，促使一百一十五個國家政府成立了專門負責環保工作的單位。1992年在巴西也舉行了第二屆地球高峰會議，目的即是要解決目前地球面臨的最大危機——地球溫度升高、森林濫伐等等嚴重的

問題。

　　人人在注意這個大問題時，其實該捫心自問，我是不是每天製造髒亂的垃圾呢？從小處著手，家庭、學校是最理想推行環保觀念的重鎮[25]。父母師長以身作則，隨時都灌輸一些環保常識，天天耳濡目染，自然而然會知道如何使垃圾分類；如何作資源回收；如何勸導愛惜物資，節省電力；如何保護樹木；以及如何避免破壞大自然的生態景觀[26]。

　　總之，不論高階層會議討論也好，家庭學校推行也好，我們每個人當然都應有一份神聖[27]的使命——環保工作從自己做起。所以說，人人都是環保尖兵。

一、生詞：New Vocabulary:

1. 清醒 qīngxǐng

   SV/AT: to be sane, clear-headed; to come to one's senses; to regain consciousness

   在頭腦清醒的時候念書最有效果。

   One gets the best results reading a book when one is clear-headed.

2. 認錯 rèncuò　**VO: to admit a fault; to admit a mistake**

   如果做錯了事，就該認錯。

   If one makes a mistake then one should admit the fault.

3. 刻意 kèyi

   A: to do something with very close attention (in order to

achieve perfection or success); to painstakingly strive for perfection or success

每次外出，她都刻意打扮一番。

Everytime she goes out, she takes the time to painstakingly deck herself out.

4. 清澈 qīngchè *SV/AT*: **to be crystal-clear (of water)**

我們坐在湖邊，看見清澈的湖水裡有雲和樹的倒影。

We sit on the lake bank and see the reflections of clouds and trees in the lake's crystal-clear water.

5. 揚波 yángpō *AT*: **to swell with waves (like the ocean)**

死水不能揚波。

Stagnant water can not swell with waves.

6. 青翠 qīngcùi *AT*: **to be fresh and green**

近的山很青翠，遠的山是藍色的。

The nearby mountains are fresh and green, the far off mountains are indigo.

7. 茂密 màomì *SV/AT*: **to be dense, thick**

她的頭髮很茂密。她有一頭茂密的黑髮。

Her hair is very thick. She has a head of thick black hair.

8. 森林 sēnlín *N*: **forest**

9. 濫伐 lànfá

V: **to log excessively, to cut down too many trees, to excessively fell trees**

濫伐山上的樹是有罪的。

To excessively fell the frees on the mountain is a crime.

10. 乾枯 gānkū

   ***SV/AT*: to be dried up, to be withered; dried up, withered**

   這棵樹乾枯了，不知道是什麼原因。

   This tree is withered; the cause is unknown.

11. 荒山 huāngshān　***N*: a barren hill; a desolate mountain**

12. 清幽 qīngyōu　***AT/SV*: quiet and secluded**

   鄉下的環境清幽，所以很多人喜歡住在鄉下。

   The surroundings of the countryside are quiet and secluded; therefore many people like to live in the countryside.

13. 原野 yuányě　***N*: a plain, a field**

14. 濃煙 nóngyān　***N*: thick smoke, dense smoke**

15. 廢氣 fèiqì

   ***N*: waste emissions (gas), gaseous wastes, waste fumes**

16. 潺潺 chánchán　***A/SV/AT*: to murmur, babble, purl**

   小河潺潺地流著，日夜不停。

   The small river murmuringly flows day and night without stopping.

17. 溪流 xīliú　***N*: a mountain stream**

18. 混濁 hǔnzhúo

   ***SV/AT*: to be muddy, turbid, not clean or pure**

   下過大雨後，清澈的河水變得混濁了。

   After a big storm the crystal-clear water of the river becomes muddy.

19. 臭溝 chòugōu　*N*: a gutter, a stinking ditch

20. 臭氧層 chòuyǎngcéng　*N*: the ozone layer

21. 破網 pòwǎng

　　N: (literally: a broken net), a ruined network, a damaged

　　system, a damaged resource

22. 紫外線 zǐwàixiàn　*N*: ultraviolet rays

23. 嬌嫩 jiāonèn

　　SV/AT: to be fragile, delicate, tender; young and tender

　　新長出來的枝葉很嬌嫩。

　　Newly budding leaves are very fragile.

24. 皮膚 pífū　*N*: skin

　　嬰兒的皮膚很嬌嫩。

　　An infant's skin is very tender.

25. 重鎮 zhòngzhèn　*N*: a key position or location

26. 景觀 jǐngguān　*N*: a view, a scene, the scenery

27. 神聖 shénshèng　*SV/AT*: to be sacred, holy, divine

　　教育工作是很神聖的。

　　Educational work is very sacred.

二、成語與俗語：Proverbs and Common Sayings:

1. 罪魁禍首 zùikúihùoshǒu

chief offender, chief criminal, archcriminal

　　這條河變色了，而且發出臭味，我們要找出罪魁禍首來。

　　This river has changed color; moreover it is giving off a

foul smell. We want to search for the chief offender.

2. 死氣沉沉 sǐqìchénchén

lifeless air, hopeless and gloomy, dull and despondent, dead atmosphere

這家公司死氣沉沉的，大概快要關門（倒閉）了。

This company has a lifeless air to it; probably it is going out of business.

3. 烏煙瘴氣 wūyānzhàngqì

(said of air) heavily polluted

抽煙的人太多，把這間休息室弄得烏煙瘴氣。

There are too many people smoking cigarettes, they have heavily polluted (the air) in this lounge.

4. 獨一無二 dúyīwúèr

unique; the one and only

他是本校獨一無二的神槍手。

He is our school's one and only marksman.

5. 慘不忍睹 cǎnbùrěndǔ

so tragic that one cannot bear to look at it

車禍現場慘不忍睹。

The scene of the auto accident was so tragic that one could not bear to look at it.

6. 百孔千瘡 bǎikǒngqiānchuāng

riddled with holes, honeycombed with holes, in very bad shape, in a state of ruin or extreme distress

戰爭後，許多房子百孔千瘡，得修理以後才能住。

After the war many homes were in a state of ruin; they had to be repaired before they could be lived in.

7. 登高一呼 dēnggāoyīhū

to raise a cry for something, to raise a hue and cry

救濟窮人，經他登高一呼，起來響應的人很多。

Relieving the poor caused him to raise a cry to which many people responded.

8. 捫心自問 ménxīnzìwèn

to examine oneself, introspection, to ask oneself

我們要捫心自問對自己的家庭，對自己的國家付出了多少？

We need to ask ourselves how much we are willing to give to our own families and to our country.

9. 小處著手 xiǎochùzhúoshǒu

To start with the details, to start with the little things (in making an analysis or resolving a problem), to not lose sight of the task at hand

我們應該從大處著眼，小處著手。

We should make an overall assessment but we must start from the details.

10. 以身作則 yǐshēnzùozé

to set an example by one's own actions (usually said of people holding responsible positions or heads of families)

父母要以身作則，才會有好的兒女。

Parents should set an example by their own actions, then they will have good children.

11. 耳濡目染 ěrrúmùrǎn

to be thoroughly influenced or imbued with what one frequently sees and hears

年輕人常和一群壞朋友在一起，耳濡目染，容易變壞。

Young people that are often together with a bad group of friends are influenced by what they see and hear and easily can become bad themselves.

12. 自然而然 ziránérrán

natural consequences, a matter of course

多聽、多看、多說，自然而然你的中文程度就提高了。

Hearing more, reading more and speaking more, it is a matter of course that the level of your Chinese has increased.

三、句型：Sentence Patterns:

1. ……因……變得（SV）

......because of......has become (SV) ...... ;

......as a result of......has become (SV) ......

(1) 他因失業，脾氣變得很壞。

(2) 空氣因下雨變得乾淨了。

(3) 爸爸因戒煙，身體變得比以前健康得多了。

2.……因……變成（N）

......as a result of......has changed to（N）......；

......because of......has become（N）......

(1) 樹上的葉子因天氣冷了，變成紅的或黃的。

(2) 他最近因每天喝很多的酒，變成了一個酒鬼。

(3) 他倆因興趣相同，變成了好朋友。

*3.*怎不令人（SV）

how can't it make one......；

how can it fail to make one......

(1) 他不想念書了，怎不令人難過呢？

(2) 她畢業了，又找到了好工作，怎不令人高興呢？

(3) 那個人亂丟垃圾，怎不令人生氣呢？

*4.*不論……也好，……也好，……都……

No matter A......or B......either of them......

(1) 不論香的花也好，不香的花也好，我都喜歡。

(2) 不論看電影也好，逛街也好，我都有時間。

(3) 不論中菜也好，西菜也好，她都會做。

四、一字多用：Single characters with multiple uses:

1. 濫伐：不可濫伐樹木。

to log excessively:

You can not excessively log trees.

濫交：濫交朋友必有惡果。

to make friends indiscriminately:

indescriminately making friends must have evil consequences.

氾濫：這條河常常氾濫。

to overflow:

This river often overflows.

濫竽充數：雖然我們合唱團的人數太少，但也不願找一些不會
　　　　　唱歌的人來濫竽充數。

to hold a post without the necessary qualifications just to make

up the number:

Although there are few people in our singing group, we also do

not look for people who cannot sing just to boost our number.

2. 清幽：她住的地方很清幽。

quiet and secluded:

The place where she lives is very quiet and secluded.

幽雅：這家咖啡館很幽雅。

quiet and elegant:

This coffee shop is very elegant.

幽默：他常常說幽默的話。 他很幽默。

humorous, humor:

He often says humorous things. He is very humorous.

3. 水溝：鄉下的水溝比較乾淨。

a ditch, a drain, a gutter:

Ditches in the countryside are cleaner.

溝通：我和他的語言很難溝通。

to bring about unobstructed exchange of (feelings, ideas, etc.), to communicate:

Without language (ability) it is hard he for and I to communicate.

代溝：你和父母之間有代溝嗎？

generation gap:

Is there a generation gap between you and your parents?

4. 魁首：這次比賽的結果誰是魁首？

leader, chief, head:

Who was the leader in the competition this time?

魁偉：他的身體魁偉。

big and tall:

His body (physique) is big and tall.

5. 廢水：每個工廠都應妥善處理廢水。

waste water:

Every factory should appropriately of waste water dispose.

廢除：不好的制度應該廢除。

to abolish, to cancel, to annul, to repeal, to rescind, to discontinue:

A bad system should be abolished.

廢話：大家都討厭廢話太多的人。

a meaningless remark, a foolish statement, a superfluous statement, rubbish:

Everybody is disgusted by people who make too many foolish statements.

廢寢忘食：他學習一種新事物的時候，常常廢寢忘食。

so absorbed (in a pursuit) as to neglect sleeping and eating:

When he studies a thing he often becomes so absorbed that he

neglects sleeping and eating.

6. 嚴重：他的病情很嚴重。

serious, grave, severe (said of an illness, situation, etc.):

The condition of his illness is very serious.

嚴厲：那所學校嚴厲處罰違規吸煙的人。

strict, stern, stringent, severe, ruthless:

That school severely punishes people who disobey the rules by

smoking.

嚴格：這個公司對員工請假的規定很嚴格。

strict, stringent:

This company is very strict about rules for workers taking time

off.

嚴肅：我的老師很嚴肅。

serious, solemn, serious-looking:

My teacher is very serious-looking.

五、問題討論：Questions for Discussion:

1. 地球為什麼不再美麗了？

_____

2. 為什麼紫外線會直接傷害到我們的皮膚？

_____

3. 什麼時候世界各國成立專門負責環保的單位？

_____

4. 第二屆地球高峰會議在何時何地舉行？目的是什麼？

_____

5. 如何推行環保？環保的常識包括哪些？

_____

6. 為什麼說人人都是環保尖兵？

_____

六、練習：Practice Exercises:

1. 選擇相反詞：

Select the word with the opposite meaning:

(1) 清　　醒____　　a.迷糊　　　b.清楚

(2) 刻　　意____　　a.有意　　　b.無心

(3) 茂　　密____　　a.茂盛　　　b.稀疏

(4) 乾　　枯____　　a.濕潤　　　b.清涼

(5) 寬　　廣____　　a.狹窄　　　b.細心

(6) 混　　濁____　　a.清靜　　　b.清澈

(7) 嬌　　嫩____　　a.粗糙　　　b.細緻

(8) 死氣沉沉____　　a.生意盎然　b.夕陽西下

(9) 百孔千瘡____　　a.破壞無遺　b.完整無缺

(10) 以身作則____　　a.以身試法　b.作賊心虛

2. 填字並解釋：

Add the correct characters and then define the following pro-
verbs:

(1) ＿＿魁＿＿首：＿＿＿＿＿＿＿＿＿＿＿＿＿＿＿＿＿＿

(2) ＿＿氣＿＿沉：＿＿＿＿＿＿＿＿＿＿＿＿＿＿＿＿＿＿

(3) ＿＿煙＿＿氣：＿＿＿＿＿＿＿＿＿＿＿＿＿＿＿＿＿＿

(4) ＿＿不＿＿睹：＿＿＿＿＿＿＿＿＿＿＿＿＿＿＿＿＿＿

(5) ＿＿孔＿＿瘡：＿＿＿＿＿＿＿＿＿＿＿＿＿＿＿＿＿＿

(6) ＿＿身＿＿則：＿＿＿＿＿＿＿＿＿＿＿＿＿＿＿＿＿＿

(7) ＿＿心＿＿問：＿＿＿＿＿＿＿＿＿＿＿＿＿＿＿＿＿＿

(8) ＿＿濡＿＿染：＿＿＿＿＿＿＿＿＿＿＿＿＿＿＿＿＿＿

(9) ＿＿高＿＿呼：＿＿＿＿＿＿＿＿＿＿＿＿＿＿＿＿＿＿

(10) ＿＿一＿＿二：＿＿＿＿＿＿＿＿＿＿＿＿＿＿＿＿＿＿

3. 有關環保問題，請回答：

Please answer the following questions about environmental protection:

(1) 你在公共場所抽煙嗎？什麼地方？

＿＿＿＿＿＿＿＿＿＿＿＿＿＿＿＿＿＿＿＿＿＿＿＿＿

(2) 你開車時，你的汽車冒黑煙嗎？嚴重不嚴重？

＿＿＿＿＿＿＿＿＿＿＿＿＿＿＿＿＿＿＿＿＿＿＿＿＿

(3) 你常用什麼容器裝食物？塑膠袋或是保麗龍盒？

＿＿＿＿＿＿＿＿＿＿＿＿＿＿＿＿＿＿＿＿＿＿＿＿＿

(4) 你喜歡哪些易開罐的飲料呢？

＿＿＿＿＿＿＿＿＿＿＿＿＿＿＿＿＿＿＿＿＿＿＿＿＿

(5) 你嚼過的口香糖吐在什麼地方？

＿＿＿＿＿＿＿＿＿＿＿＿＿＿＿＿＿＿＿＿＿＿＿＿＿

(6) 你用過什麼樣的再生紙？

＿＿＿＿＿＿＿＿＿＿＿＿＿＿＿＿＿＿＿＿＿＿＿＿＿

(7) 你玩過媽媽用舊衣服做的布玩偶嗎？

(8) 你平常做垃圾分類嗎？分幾類？

閱讀與探討
Read and Discuss

短篇廣播劇——山明水秀

劇中人

于世川（父）：化工廠的董事長

于曉青（青）：于世川的女兒

黃經田（黃）：于世川的朋友

陳鴻昌（陳）：化工廠的廠長

（一）

父：在美國教書的那位黃叔叔要回來了？

青：噢，好啊！

父：他打算回來半個月，要到各地去走走看看。我約好他，在這兒的時候呢，就住在我們家。他毫不猶豫地就答應了。

青：他跟爸爸是小時候的玩伴。長大以後，又成了好朋友。既然到這兒，他哪會不住在我們家呢？

父：你倒是挺了解的啊！

（二）

黃：世川啊！想不到你還真會享福啊！

父：你這話怎麼說啊？

青：黃叔叔的意思是不是說，我們選了一個很好的住家環境？

黃：欸！對！小青的腦袋可真靈活。世川啊！你這棟別墅，蓋在半山腰上，面對基隆河，可以說是有山有水啊！

青：是啊！黃叔叔，我們這兒視野開闊，白天可以看到基隆河的水流波光，晚上可以欣賞到整個大都市像銀河一般的夜景，住起來真是舒服！

父：這也不能叫享福啊！哎！我問你，一個人大半輩子辛辛苦苦賺錢，為了什麼？

黃：你這問題範圍太大了。

父：當然是改善生活嘛！啊！論吃的方面，一個人的胃畢竟有限。剩下來就是住的，既然有這份能力，當然要找個好的環境住嘛！

黃：的確，這麼大的一個庭院，加上有一個獨立的車庫，有錢還不見得買得到呢！

父：主要是從這兒去我的化工廠很方便，開車五分鐘就到了。

青：咦！這是什麼味道？好臭喔！爸，黃叔叔，你們聞到了沒有？

黃、父：聞到了！聞到了！

青：奇怪，這股臭味哪來的呢？

父：我們從前沒聞過啊！

青：啊！我懂了！我們才搬過來一個多月。爸經常不在家，而且一回到了家，就躲在房間裡。門窗關著，開冷氣，當然聞不到了啊！

父：這麼說來，你常常聞到嘍？

青：可是臭味沒今晚這麼濃。或許是風向的關係，而且又在頂樓陽臺

上。

父：哎喲！真是臭得不得了！經田，小心！我們進裡邊去吧！

黃：好。

（三）

父：這位黃先生是我小時候的老友。你帶他到處去看看。把廠裡的情況，給他做個詳細的介紹。

陳：好的，董事長。

父：經田啊！對不起呀！碰巧有一個難纏的客戶，非得我親自跟他見面不可。只好暫時的勞駕陳廠長了。

黃：你忙你的。

父：那我就失陪了。

陳：噢！黃先生，你有沒有特別想看的地方？

黃：這樣吧，我想先看看廠裡邊廢水處理的情形。

陳：好，那我就陪你從那兒開始看。

（四）

青：黃叔叔，我給你泡茶來了。

黃：謝謝。曉青啊！這杯茶，該不會用基隆河的水泡的吧？

青：好噁心喲！你怎麼這麼說呢？我一想到基隆河裡邊的水，就噁心的想吐！

黃：為什麼呢？

青：因為它髒得像墨水啊！而且到處是垃圾。才搬來那天啊，我興沖沖地跑到河邊去散步，給嚇得以後都不敢再去了。

黃：世川啊！曉青說的情形，你可曾注意過沒有？

父：沒有啊！我忙著做生意賺錢，哪來這些閒工夫啊？

黃：老朋友啊！這就不對啦！

父：為什麼啊？

黃：賺錢固然重要，多留意身邊的事物更重要。昨天晚上我們都領教了空氣裡邊的那股臭味，可是你們父女倆可曾進一步去了解，它是從哪兒來的嗎？

父、女：沒有啊！

黃：這就對啦！我告訴你們，那股臭味就是從基隆河裡邊冒上來的。

父、女：真的啊！

黃：當然是真的啊！因為我是研究生態保育的，對這方面的問題特別的用心，也特別的敏感。世川，我再請問你，你可知道你廠裡的廢水都排放到哪裡去了嗎？

父：當然是基隆河啊！當初在那兒設廠，考慮的就是這點啊！

黃：很方便是不是？你可知道，我們昨天晚上聞到那股臭味，你也是造成的兇手之一。

父：啊？我？

黃：因為我仔細看過了。你那個工廠的廢水，完全沒有經過污水處理就放出去。那會對我們自然環境，造成嚴重的傷害。

父：哎呀！我那個工廠那麼小，一天才排放多少廢水嘛！

黃：你這種觀念啊！真是害人害己。哪怕是丟一張廢紙，都會污染環境。所以人人都應該在觀念上建立共識，在行為上改正從前亂丟垃圾的壞習慣，來共同維護良好衛生的自然環境。

青：黃叔叔說的很有道理。

黃：曉青啊！你知道嗎？我們小時候，這附近的基隆河、新美溪、蘭溪，都可以游泳、釣魚、划船呢！

青：好棒噢！如果現在還能這樣，不知道有多好！

黃：對！只要我們大家同心協力，絕對有那麼一天的！

問答：Answer the following questions:

1. 黃叔叔回來半個月，為什麼毫不猶豫地答應住在曉青家？

_____

2. 如果不住在曉青家，還可能住在哪兒？

_____

3. 為什麼黃叔叔說曉青的腦袋真靈活？

_____

4. 黃叔叔怎麼說曉青爸爸很會享福？

_____

5. 曉青父親為什麼選這個地方蓋別墅？

_____

6. 為什麼曉青父親聞不到那股臭味？

_____

7. 黃叔叔跟陳廠長說他特別想看什麼地方？

_____

8. 為什麼曉青都不敢到河邊去散步？

_____

9. 在曉青家聞到的臭味到底怎麼來的？

_____

10. 我們應該怎麼去共同維護良好衛生的自然環境？

_____

第十課　春　節

　　再過兩天學校就要開始放一個月的聖誕假了，王小美在校園中剛好碰見他的中國朋友李台生。

美：台生，好久不見，你好嗎？還有課沒有？

生：還不錯，現在沒課了。

美：那好極了！我們就在這兒坐下聊一聊吧！

生：後天學校開始放假，你有什麼計畫？

美：我打算回家跟家人一塊過節。說到過節，我想問你一個問題，在中國有沒有像聖誕節這樣特別重要的節日？

生：當然有啦！中國人最重要的節日是「過年①」，也就是「春節②」。正式活動是從臘月③二十三到正月④十七。臘月一開始，大街小巷充滿了過年的氣氛，這種氣氛會持續⑤一個半月之久。

美：你剛才說的「臘月」和「正月」是什麼意思？

生：「臘」是祭祖⑥的意思。臘祭在陰曆⑦十二月舉行，所以叫「臘月」。「正月」就是陰曆的第一個月，正月的第一天春天開始，所以又叫「春節」。

美：為什麼說正式活動從二十三號開始？

生：因為臘月二十三這天，傳說是灶神⑧升天⑨的日子，這天也叫「過小年」。除了把廚房打掃乾淨以外，還得請他吃糖，這樣他向天帝報告這家的情形，就都會說好話，而讓這家一年生活順利。這天之後，各家就忙著打掃、整理內外、辦年貨等，積極準備過年。

美：為什麼叫「過年」？

生：傳說「年」這個字，古代是指一個兇惡⑩的怪獸⑪，平常住在深山裡，每年到了除夕⑫晚上出來，到處傷人。牠怕紅色，看到紅色大門的人家，就過門不入。於是，大家在屋裡一夜不敢睡覺叫「守歲」⑬。深夜一到十二點以後，家家戶戶接二連三放鞭炮⑭來嚇走「年」。一到天亮就是正月初一，凡是跟你見面的人，你都說恭喜⑮，意思是還好你沒被年傷到。

美：「除夕」是什麼意思？

生：「除夕」是指一年的最後一天，有除去舊年迎接⑯新年的意思。這天大家忙著貼春聯⑰、祭祖、放鞭炮、吃年夜飯⑱（團圓⑲飯）。飯後，向長輩拜年領壓歲錢⑳。近午夜的時候，吃元寶㉑（餃子㉒）、守歲。

美：正月初一這天做什麼呢？

生：正月初一就是元旦㉓，大家穿上新衣，互相拜年㉔，見面說恭喜。在春節期間，你要多說吉利㉕話。如果你打破了東西，就馬上說歲歲（碎碎）平安。

美：正月裡有沒有別的熱鬧日子？

生：最後一個春節歡樂的高潮㉖是正月十五的「元宵節㉗」。這
　　天到處張燈結綵、玩花燈㉘、猜燈謎㉙、吃元宵（湯圓㉚）
　　十分熱鬧。現在，政府已經把這個能充分發揮㉛民族才藝
　　的日子定為觀光節㉜了。對不起，我還有個約，得先走
　　了，今天就說到這兒，下次有空再聊，再見！

美：再見！

一、生詞：New Vocabulary:

1. 過年 guònián

   VO: the Chinese New Year; to celebrate the Chinese New
   Year

   孩子們都喜歡過年。

   Children all love to celebrate the Chinese New Year.

2. 春節 chūnjié　　**N**: the Spring Festival

3. 臘月 làyuè

   N: the twelfth month of the Chinese Lunar year

4. 正月 zhèngyuè

   N: the first month of the Chinese lunar year

5. 持續 chíxù　　**A**: continuous, incesssant, uninterrupted

   持續下了十天的雨，大家都希望馬上看見太陽。

   It has continuously rained for ten days; everbody wishes to
   immediately see the sun.

6. 祭祖 jìzǔ

   VO: to perform rites in honor of one's ancestors

   過年過節的時候，許多家庭都在祭祖。

   When celebrating the Chinese New Year, many families perform the rites honoring their ancestors.

7. 陰曆 yīnlì

   N: the Chinese lunar calendar; a calendar based on the cycles of the moon

8. 灶神 zàushén

   N: the Kitchen God, the God of the Kitchen

9. 升天 shēngtiān

   N: to ascend to heaven; to transmigrate; to die

   人死了會升天嗎？

   Can the dead ascend to heaven?

10. 兇惡 (兇＝凶) xiōngè

    SV/AT: to be wicked; evil; savage; malignant

    他夢見一隻凶惡的野獸正要咬他，結果他嚇醒了。

    He dreamed that a savage beast was about to bite him; as a result, he was frightened awake.

11. 怪獸 guàishòu

    N: a legendary animal; a rare animal; a monster

12. 除夕 chúxì　**N: Chinese New Year's Eve**

13. 守歲 shǒusùi

    VO: to see the old year out and to welcome the new year in

by staying up on the night of Chinese New Year's Eve.

除夕大家都在守歲，可是小孩子守著守著都睡著了。

On Chinese New Year's Eve everybody stays up to see out the old year and welcome in the new year, but the children wait and wait and then all fall asleep.

14. 鞭炮 biānpào   *N*: **firecrackers**

15. 恭喜 gōngxǐ   *VO*: **congratulations**

過年時，一見到人就說「恭喜，恭喜」。

During Chinese New Year, when one meets another person, they should say "congratulations, congratulations".

16. 迎接 yíngjiē   *V*: **to meet; to greet**

迎接新年到來，第一件要做的事，就是放鞭炮。

To greet the coming New Year, the first thing to do is to set off firecrackers.

17. 春聯 chūnlián

N: **The New Year's couplets written on strips of red paper and pasted on door frames. These couplets usually contain words of luck.**

18. 年夜飯 niányèfàn

N: **The special dinner eaten on the eve of the Chinese New Year**

19. 團圓 tuányuán   *N*: **a reunion (of family, etc.)**

20. 壓歲錢 yāsuiqián

N: **cash given in red paper envelopes to children by their**

elders on the eve of the Chinese New Year

21. 元宝 yuánbǎo

N: **a type of dumpling made in a shape reminiscent of the silver and gold ingots once used as money in ancient China**

22. 餃子 jiǎozi　*N*: **dumplings**

23. 元旦 yuándàn　*N*: **Chinese New Year's day**

24. 拜年 bàinián

VO: **to pay a respectful call on relatives or friends on New Year's Day and offer New Year's greetings**

現在流行電話拜年。

It is now popular to make a phone call to extend one's New Year greetings.

25. 吉利 jílì　*SV/AT*: **to be lucky, auspicious, propitious**

過年時一定要多說吉利的話。

During the Chinese New Year one should say a lot of auspicious things.

26. 高潮 gāocháo　*N*: **the climax; the upsurge**

27. 元宵節 yuánxiāojié　*N*: **The Lantern Festival**

28. 花燈 huādēng

N: **fancy lanterns (usually made of paper) made especially for the Lantern Festival.**

29. 燈謎 dēngmí

N: **riddles which are written on lanterns (used in contests** in which prizes are often offered)

30. 湯ㄊㄤ圓ㄩㄢˊ tāngyuán

　　N: balls made of glutinous- rice flour (often filled with a sweet paste)

31. 發ㄈㄚ揮ㄏㄨㄟ fāhūi

　　V: to bring (a skill or talent) into full play; to give play to (a skill, talent, etc.)

　　我們要發揮愛心，救濟災民。

　　We want to bring love into play in providing relief to the disaster victims.

32. 觀ㄍㄨㄢ光ㄍㄨㄤ節ㄐㄧㄝˊ guānguāngjié

　　N: a sightseeing holiday; a holiday aimed at tourists and tourism

二、成語與俗語：Proverbs and Common Sayings:

1. 大ㄉㄚˋ街ㄐㄧㄝ小ㄒㄧㄠˇ巷ㄒㄧㄤˋ dàjiēxiǎoxiàng

in every street and alley, all over the city

　　這幾天大街小巷都有人放鞭炮。

　　These past few days people have been setting off firecrackers all over the city.

2. 家ㄐㄧㄚ家ㄐㄧㄚ戶ㄏㄨˋ戶ㄏㄨˋ jiājiāhùhù

every family and household

　　過年時，家家戶戶都要吃年糕。

　　During the Chinese New Year, every family and household

wants to eat the special New Year's glutinous rice cakes.

3. 接二連三 jiēèrliánsān

continuously, one after another, repeatedly

這個工廠接二連三發生了幾件不幸的事。

This factory has continuously had bad things occur.

4. 歲歲（碎碎）平安 suìsuìpíngān

a play on words (a pun) which literally means "smashed safe and sound" but can also be heard to mean "safe and sound year after year".

過年時，打破了任何東西都要趕緊說「歲歲（碎碎）平安。」

During the Chinese New Year, if one breaks anything, she/ he should hasten to say "safe and sound year after year".

5. 張燈結綵 zhāngdēngjiécǎi

to be decorated with lanterns and colored hangings (for a joyous occasion)

從前結婚時都要張燈結綵。

In the past the occasion of marriage called for decorations of lanterns and colored hangings.

三、句型： Sentence Patterns:

1. 凡是……都

every...... (all) ...... ;

all......are (all) ...... ;

any...... (all) ......

(1) 凡是認識他的人都喜歡他。

(2) 凡是我買的書都是好書。

(3) 凡是剛喝過酒的人都不該開車。

2. 把······定為

......to set......as the date for......

......to appoint......as the time for......

(1) 政府把孔子的生日定為教師節。

(2) 學校把學期的最後一個禮拜定為考期。

(3) 父母把每月的第一個禮拜六晚上定為家庭團聚的日子。

四、練習：Practice Exercises:

1. 解釋下列詞語：

Define the following terms:

(1) 祭祖：＿＿＿＿＿＿＿＿＿＿＿＿＿＿＿＿

(2) 守歲：＿＿＿＿＿＿＿＿＿＿＿＿＿＿＿＿

(3) 吉利話：＿＿＿＿＿＿＿＿＿＿＿＿＿＿＿

(4) 升天：＿＿＿＿＿＿＿＿＿＿＿＿＿＿＿＿

(5) 辦年貨：＿＿＿＿＿＿＿＿＿＿＿＿＿＿＿

(6) 傷人：＿＿＿＿＿＿＿＿＿＿＿＿＿＿＿＿

(7) 拜年：＿＿＿＿＿＿＿＿＿＿＿＿＿＿＿＿

(8) 深夜：＿＿＿＿＿＿＿＿＿＿＿＿＿＿＿＿

2. 選同音的字，畫一條線：

Select and underline the character with the same pronunciation:

例：　聖：神　成　勝　取

(1) 誕：但　延　談　沿

(2) 聊：了　柳　仰　遼

(3) 臘：獵　辣　拉　來

(4) 祭：記　登　其　奇

(5) 升：省　生　盛　井

(6) 淨：掙　景　境　經

(7) 凶：雄　亞　比　兄

(8) 鞭：邊　便　遍　變

(9) 宵：笑　小　消　雲

(10) 嚇：下　黑　赤　之

3.填空：

Fill in the blanks:

(1) 臘是_____的意思。陰曆_____月舉行，所以叫臘月。

(2) 正月是陰曆的第____個月，正月的第一天春天開始，所以又叫_____。

(3) 臘月_____傳說是_____升天的日子。

(4) _____是指一年的最後一天，忙著____春聯，____祖，放_____吃_____。

(5) 正月____一就是_____，大家互相____。

(6) 春節期間多說_____話。如果打破了東西馬上說_____。

(7) 正月十五是_____。大家猜____，吃_____。政府已經把這個節定為_____節了。

4.選擇相似的詞語：

Select the word with a similar meaning:

(1) 持續：＿＿＿　a.連續　b.斷斷續續　c.維持

(2) 正月：＿＿＿　a.元月　b.當月　c.臘月

(3) 陰曆：＿＿＿　a.陽曆　b.農曆　c.月曆

(4) 除夕：＿＿＿　a.新年　b.元旦　c.年三十

(5) 團圓：＿＿＿　a.圓滿　b.團聚　c.圓圈

(6) 吉利：＿＿＿　a.吉祥　b.吉兆　c.吉凶

(7) 守歲：＿＿＿　a.守門　b.守夜　c.除夕不睡

(8) 元宵：＿＿＿　a.年糕　b.湯圓　c.湯包

佳文欣賞

年夜飯

子　敏

　　每年除夕，家家都要吃一頓年夜飯。準備的菜，總是那麼豐盛，足夠擺滿一桌。

　　往年，我的家也是一樣，人人對那一頓豐盛的年夜飯，都有濃濃的興趣。記得去年，我就是第一個對孩子們的媽媽預訂菜碼的人。

　　我說：「有兩道菜我是一定要的。第一，是豌豆仁兒炒蝦仁。這是我最愛吃的。年夜飯吃不到這一道菜，就像缺少了甚麼似的。第二，是一大碗清燉雞湯。雞肉要細嫩一點兒的，我喜歡拿雞肉蘸醬油吃。雞湯味道鮮美，過年更是不能不喝。小時候在家鄉，母親知道，年夜飯我喝不到雞湯就會賭氣不吃

飯，所以忘不了再三交代廚子，不能沒有這一道湯。」

媽媽靜靜的聽著。

老大說：「媽媽，別忘了我那一大盤炒米粉，要多放一點蝦米、香菇丁兒，還有肉絲。就是連吃三天，我也吃不膩。」

老二說：「媽媽，別忘了做一鍋滷雞翅膀。啃雞翅膀，真是越啃越香，就算沒有別的菜，我也夠了。」

媽媽靜靜的聽著。

老三說：「我最想吃的是炸丸子。豬肉丸子和素菜丸子，兩樣都要。還有，咖哩豬肉加馬鈴薯，這也是我要的。我要拿來拌飯吃。」

媽媽靜靜的聽著。

除夕的前兩天，媽媽打掃屋子已經夠累的了，但是不得不再提起精神，到中央市場去買菜。她邀老大跟我去幫忙。她說：「要買的東西夠多的了。你們幫我到市場裡去守著一個據點。我買了東西就往你們這邊送，等一切都買齊了，大家再一起提回家。」

那一天，我們整整用去一個上午的時間，好不容易才把菜買齊，回到家裡，已經累得連動都不想動了。

今年，在除夕的前幾天，我在家裡聽到了跟往年不同的聲音。說話的是老大。

她說：「我們想的是甚麼菜好吃，受累的是媽媽。去年吃年夜飯，媽媽雖然跟我們坐在一起，但是甚麼都吃不下，只喝

了半杯開水。」

　　老二說：「改變改變吧！」

　　今年的年夜飯，飯桌上出現一個電爐，爐上是一鍋開水。電爐的四周，擺滿了老大買回來的各式各樣的火鍋食品。媽媽沒上菜市場，也沒為了做那十幾道菜，從中午忙到傍晚。她跟大家一起吃火鍋，而且說了一句大家聽了都很開心的話：「今年過年，好像比往年有意思多了！」

第十一課　強化體質①

劇中人

王太太 (王)：大明的母親
王大明 (明)：國中二年級的學生
林醫生 (林)：一家私立醫院院長

明：咳！咳！咳！（一陣咳嗽聲）

王：大夫，為什麼這孩子的體質總是比別人差，動不動就感冒了呢？

林：其實體質的強弱是父母給的，無法自行選擇。就像皮膚被蚊子②咬了，有的人擦了藥，依然紅腫③潰爛④，有的卻不管他，反而平安無事。

王：說實在的，我還不完全明白體質的意思，你可不可以給我解釋一下？

林：體質就是身體強弱的性質，體質強的抵抗力⑤也強；體質弱的抵抗力也弱。平常體質可分成乾性、濕性和中性三類。乾性體質，皮膚乾燥不易過敏⑥，感冒時只咳嗽，不打噴嚏⑦；濕性體質剛好相反；中性體質，介於乾性和濕性之間，兩種特性互相出現。認清了自己是哪一種體質，

保養方法是隨著季節、氣候、溫度、濕度等環境因素⑧而加減衣服，少吃不利於體質的食物、藥物等。二十世紀由於食品添加物⑨、農藥⑩等化學藥品越來越普遍使用，使得人們在先天⑪遺傳⑫過敏性體質外，又增加了後天容易過敏的因素。

王：那這種後天因素怎麼避免呢？

林：可以從小環境——家庭做起。父母不要過度⑬保護孩子，孩子咳一聲就加一件衣服，咳兩聲就加兩件，其實這樣做，只會產生惡性⑭循環⑮。聰明的父母在孩子感冒好了以後，帶他出去從事戶外活動，這樣強化體質(即創造⑯後天⑰體質)之後，衣服就可以少穿一點，也不必擔心他會再感冒了。

王：是不是需要吃點什麼藥，補補他的身子？

林：俗語說的好，「藥補不如食補」。其實三餐飲食正常，營養均衡⑱，不必花很多錢，絕對好過那些昂貴⑲的藥材。不要一味姑息或縱容⑳子女養成偏食㉑的習慣。病了，父母就以求仙丹㉒的心態去找醫生，其實仙丹不在醫生那兒，只有父母才有。

王：謝謝你告訴我這麼多，真是「聽君一席話，勝讀十年書」！大明，還不趕快過來，向大夫說聲謝謝！

明：謝謝林大夫。

王、明：(同聲說)再見！

林：再見！

一、生詞：New Vocabulary：

1. 體質 tǐzhíc　*N*: (physical) constitution

2. 蚊子 wénzi　*N*: mosquito

3. 紅腫 hóngzhǒng

   V/AT: red and swollen; inflammation

   他被蚊子咬的地方紅腫起來了。

   The place where he was bitten by a mosquito became red and swollen.

4. 潰爛 kùilàn

   V/AT: to fester; to ulcerate; (in a wound) to become infected

   你的手再不找醫生就潰爛了。

   If you still don't seek out a doctor, your hand will become infected.

5. 抵抗力 dǐkànglì　*N*: resistance (to disease), immunity

6. 過敏 gùomǐn　*V/AT*: allergic reaction (s) ; allergy

   鼻子過敏是很難治的病。

   Nasal allergies are hard to treat.

7. 打噴嚏 dǎpēntì　*VO*: to sneeze

   我今天早上一起床就一直打噴嚏。

   On getting up from bed this morning, I sneezed three times.

8. 因素　yīnsù　*N*: factor; element

9. 添加物 tiānjiāwù　*N*: (food, chemical) additives

10. 農藥 nóngyào　**N: pesticide, agricultural chemical**

11. 先天 xiāntiān　***AT*: congenital; innate**

有許多疾病是先天的。

Many illnesses are congenital.

12. 遺傳 yíchuán　**N: heredity; inheritance**

13. 過度 guòdù

***A*: excessive; undue; too much; over- (i.e., over-eating, over-sleeping, etc.)**

用功過度會影響健康。

Excessive diligence can affect one's health.

14. 惡性 èxìng　***AT*: malignant; pernicious; vicious**

有些貧窮家庭無法給子女受較好的教育，往往造成惡性循環。

Some poor families have no way to provide their children with a better education; this often creates a vicious circle.

15. 循環 xúnhuán

***V/N*: (*a*) to cycle, circulate**

(*b*) a cycle, circle

血液循環良好的人比較健康。

People with good blood circulation are more healthy.

16. 創造 chùangzào　***V*: to create; to produce**

她想創造一種新的藝術風格。

She wants to create a new art style.

17. 後天 hòutiān　***AT*: acquired**

後天的努力才是成功的要素。

Acquired diligence is an essential factor for success.

18. 均衡 jūnhéng

AT/N: (a) balanced; harmonious; proportionate; even

　　(b) equality, equilibrium, a balance (of power, etc.)

營養不可過多，也不可不夠，最重要的是力求均衡。

One should not have too much nourishment, nor should one have not enough; it is most important to strive for a balance.

19. 昂貴 ángguì　**AT/SV: costly, very expensive**

昂貴的東西不一定是合適的東西。

Costly things are not necessarily the right things.

20. 縱容 zòngróng

V: to pass over indulgently, to make less of something than one should; to connive at, to wink at

有縱容自己的兒子跟別人打架的父母嗎？

Are there parents who indulgently pass over the fact that their own sons are getting into brawls with others?

21. 偏食 piānshí

AT/N: to be picky in eating; picky eating habits; to only be willing to eat certain dishes (usually said of children)

小孩兒偏食是父母頭痛的問題。

Children being picky in their eating habits is a problem which gives (their) parents headaches.

22. 仙丹 xiāndān　**N: a panacea, a miracle cure, a cure-all**

二、成語與俗語：Proverbs and Common Sayings:

1. 平安無事 píngānwúshì

   safe and sound; safe and without any mishaps; in good order

   > 這次地震，我們全家平安無事，真是幸運！

   We are really lucky; in the earthquake this time, our whole family came out safe and sound.

2. 藥補不如食補 yàobǔbùrúshíbǔ

   The benefits of medicine are not as great as those of good nutrition

   > 吃營養的東西，不要吃補藥，因為藥補不如食補。

   Eat nutritious things, and don't take medicines, because the benefits of medicine are not as great as those of good nutrition.

   > (Note: 補藥 is any type of medicine which promotes one's health rather than curing one's illness (e.g. a health tonic)

3. 一味姑息 yíwèigūxí

   to habitually indulge in; to invariably spoil; to always be lenient

   > 父母不可一味姑息子女。

   Parents can't always be lenient with their children.

4. 聽君一席話，勝讀十年書

   tīngjūnyìxíhuà, shèngdúshíniánshū

listening to the words of a wise man can be superior to studying ten years worth of books

今天聽了李教授的演講，大家都覺得收穫頗豐，真是「聽君一席話，勝讀十年書」啊！

Everybody felt they gained a great deal by listening to Professor Lee's lecture today; it's true, "listening to the words of a wise man can be superior to studying ten years worth of books"!

三、句型：Sentence patterns:

1. 動不動就⋯⋯

to be apt to...... ;

to be liable to...... ;

to tend to......

(1) 她動不動就生氣。

(2) 這個小孩動不動就哭。

(3) 這對夫妻動不動就吵架。

2. 有的⋯⋯依然⋯⋯；有的⋯⋯反而⋯⋯

some... ...still...... , on the other

hand...... , others...... ;

some...... as before will ...... ,

others...... , on the contrary,

will......

(1) 冬天來了，有的樹依然翠綠，有的樹反而開花了。

(2) 下雨了，有的人依然在圖書館看書，有的人反而到游泳池去游泳了。

(3) 有的人吃很多補藥，身體依然瘦弱，有的人從來不吃補藥，身體反而很健壯。

3. 介於……之間

X lies between...... ;

X occupies a position between...... ;

X falls between......

(1) 大學教授對學生來說介於老師和朋友之間。

(2) 這種顏色介於黃和綠之間。

(3) 這個地方介於城市和鄉村之間。

4. 由於……使得……外，又……

owing to......not only is X true......but Y (has also resulted);

as the result of......not only has X occurred......but Y (has also come to pass)

(1) 他由於每天早上爬山，使得身體健康外，又交了朋友。

(2) 由於喜歡賭博，使得他失去了工作外，又欠了別人很多錢。

(3) 由於戰爭，使得許多人沒飯吃外，又沒房子住。

5. 其實……只有……才……

actually X only requires Y in order to...... ;

in fact, only Y is required for X (to be come / be true)

(1) 世界雖大，其實只有自己的家才最可愛。

(2) 他渴望成功，其實成功只有靠自己努力才能得到。

(3) 她怕感染疾病，其實疾病只有自己多注意才能避免感染。

四、易混淆的詞：Easily Confused Words：

1. 潰爛 kùilàn **SV/AT: to burst**

燙傷的皮膚，一不小心就很容易潰爛。

If one is not careful it is very easy to burst scalded (burned) skin.

潰散 kùisàn **V: to disperse; to break-up**

軍隊戰敗，潰散四處。

The defeated army dispersed in all directions (dispersed to the four winds).

崩潰 bēngkùi **V/N: to collapse**

工作壓力太大，使他精神快崩潰了。

The pressure at work is too great; it will soon cause his spirit to collapse (cause him to have a nervous breakdown).

俄國共產黨政權崩潰以後，成立很多小獨立國。

After the collapse of political power of the Russian Communist party, many small independent countries were established.

2. 過敏 gùomǐn **V/N: to be allergic**

鼻子過敏的人常愛打噴嚏。

People with nasal allergies sneeze often.

敏感 mǐngǎn **SV/AT: to be susceptible; to be sensitive**

有的人很敏感，跟他說話得小心。

Some people are very sensitive; one must be careful when talking with them.

3. 普遍 pǔbiàn

***SV/AT*: to be widespread; to be everywhere; to be common**

看電視是家庭中最普遍的娛樂。

Watching television is the most widespread (type) of household entertainment.

五十年前電視不太普遍。

Fifty years ago television was not very widespread.

普及 pǔjí

***SV/AT*: to be available to all; to be commonly available**

電視教育普及到各鄉村。

Educational television is commonly available throughout the countryside.

普通 pǔtōng

***SV/AT*: to be ordinary; to be average; to be common**

我只要普通的產品，不要特別的。

I just want ordinary products; I don't want anything special.

4. 縱容 zòngróng

***V*: to connive, to wink at, to turn a blind eye (to one breaking a rule)**

父母常縱容孩子，不加管教。

Parents often turn a blind eye to their children (to their misdeeds) and don't discipline them.

放縱 fàngzòng

***V*: to act uninhibited; to be debauched; to act disrespectfully**

太放縱孩子，容易出問題。

Children who act too uninhibited often have problems.

操ㄘㄠ縱ㄗㄨㄥ cāozòng

V/N: to manipulate (people, events, etc.); to control; to wield; to hold

在公司操縱大權的人，常喜歡控制一切。

At work people who wield authority often like to control everything.

5. 避ㄅㄧ免ㄇㄧㄢ bìmiǎn

V: to avoid; to refrain from; to avert

說話要有風度，避免得罪朋友。

When speaking one should behave with good manners and refrain from offending friends.

以ㄧ免ㄇㄧㄢ yǐmiǎn

A: (to do something) in order to avoid or prevent

把護照放在手提包內以免遺失。

Put the passport in the handbag in order to prevent it from being lost.

防ㄈㄤ止ㄓ fángzhǐ

V: to prevent; to guard against; to avoid

保持環境清潔，防止疾病傳染。

Maintaining a clean environment prevents the spread of diseases.

五、問題討論：Questions for Discussion:

1. 為什麼孩子們的體質有的強有的弱？

_____

2. 體質的強弱和抵抗力有什麼關係？

_____

3. 濕性體質的人和乾性體質的人感冒時有何不同？

_____

4. 後天容易過敏的因素有哪些？

_____

5. 孩子感冒後，父母該怎麼辦？

_____

6. 為什麼藥補不如食補？

_____

六、練習：Practice Exercises:

1. 選相似詞：(單選和複選)

Select the Phrase or Expression with the Same Meaning:

(1) 總是：____　　*a.*老是　*b.*就是　*c.*倒是

(2) 依然：____　　*a.*仍然　*b.*仍舊　*c.*還是

(3) 過度：____　　*a.*過分　*b.*適度　*c.*經過

(4) 從事：____　　*a.*從前　*b.*跟隨　*c.*做

(5) 擔心：____　　*a.*憂慮　*b.*擔憂　*c.*負擔

(6) 均衡：____　　*a.*偏重　*b.*相等　*c.*平均

(7) 縱容：____　　*a.*縱然　*b.*放縱　*c.*縱橫

(8) 偏食： ____　a.挑食　b.貪吃　c.偏愛

2.填空：

Fill in the Blanks:

(1) 體質強的_____力也強。

(2) 體質可分為_____、_____和_____三種。

(3) 俗語說：「藥補不如_____。」

(4) 孩子咳一聲就加一件衣服，咳兩聲就加兩件，其實只會產生_____循環。

(5) 三餐飲食正常，_____均衡，身體就會健康。

(6) 聽君一席話，勝讀_____。

3.造句：

Make Sentences:

(1) 因素：_____

(2) 遺傳：_____

(3) 過度：_____

(4) 均衡：_____

(5) 縱容：_____

(6) 動不動就：_____

(7) 介於……之間：_____

(8) 先天：_____

4.選擇同音字：

Select the Character with the same pronunciation:

(1) 添： ____　a.天　b.漆　c.甜

(2) 抵： ____　a.低　b.地　c.底

(3) 循： ____　a.環　b.尋　c.均

⑷ 衡：＿＿＿　　*a.*衝　*b.*橫　*c.*行

⑸ 丹：＿＿＿　　*a.*擔　*b.*但　*c.*舟

⑹ 嚏：＿＿＿　　*a.*梯　*b.*第　*c.*替

佳文欣賞

運動最補

夏承楹

　　中國人是一種講究「補」的民族，人的身體要從頭「補」到腳，從內「補」到外，總覺得人生於世，處處有「虧」，時時要「補」。

　　一般人「補」的觀念中有「藥補」和「食補」兩種。我不大相信補藥的效力，除非那是醫生推薦的。對於食補我也持保留的態度，因為有些食物吃了有益，有些卻有害。就我的經驗來說，世上最好的補品莫過於運動。從學生時代到現在，幾十年來我從沒有停止過運動，因此沒有住過一天醫院。我相信使我支持得了每週七天，每天八小時工作的主要原因是運動。人對自己的身體健康雖不必時時膽戰心驚，疑神疑鬼，也不可「恃強拒補」，妄充硬漢。故此我要在「藥補不如食補」之後加上一句：「食補不如運動補」。

　　我認為從來不運動的人可以從簡單的運動，如：慢跑、健身操等開始，漸進到有競爭性的運動，如：桌球、羽球、網

球、排球等。因為獨自做和無競爭性的運動容易令人產生枯燥、厭倦的感覺，競爭可以使人因興趣增高而持之以恆。

　　所以現代的人應將運動列為日常生活的要項，像吃飯喝茶一樣。每天運動的習慣該在學生時代養成，就業以後繼續維持下去。醫學家說，運動可以促進人體生理器官的功能，消除緊張，舒暢精神，使生活更為充實有力，因而達到延年益壽的目的。而健康長壽是生活的享受和成功的基礎，則是人所共知的。「藥補」與「食補」是沒有發現運動之益以前的說法，健康的人根本不需要「補」，而且「補」錯了反而會發生毛病。因此我根據個人經驗、專家之言和成功者的故事，提出「運動最補」之說。

～《人生於世》純文學出版社～

第十二課　談素食①

　　在熙熙攘攘的通衢②大街上，夾雜③在漢堡④、炸雞、披薩⑤……速食店⑥廣告燈中，你可能發現一些素食店的招牌，原來吃素是近年來最流行的一種生活方式。在朋友間，不論年輕人或老年人都會有一些素食者，所以如果你想請客時，也得打聽清楚後再做決定。在西餐方面，最盛行⑦的可能算是「沙拉吧⑧」了。十幾種各式各樣的蔬菜，擺滿一桌，令人垂涎三尺，自然吸引人們去大啖⑨一番，加上各式不同的佐料，如法國的美乃滋⑩、意大利的油醋，拌成天下美味，同時也攝取⑪到了人體所須的養料及維生素⑫。在中餐方面，更是花樣百出，以豆腐⑬做出的「炸丸子」，味道不遜於⑭純肉做的肉圓；以豆腐皮炸出的「香酥鴨⑮」，吃起來幾可亂真；再以香菇切絲加上配料炒出來的「炒鱔糊⑯」，色香味俱全。大快朵頤之餘，誰會料到一餐下來沒犧牲任何一條生命，心中是不是更加暢快呢！

　　中國人一向說：「青菜豆腐保平安。」這句話的意思是說，大魚大肉並不是最理想的食物，清清淡淡的蔬菜，內含豐富的各種維生素，豆類的蛋白可代替動物的蛋白，再加米麵等穀類⑰配食，是足夠人體所須的養分，而且還防止不少可致命

的疾病呢！有些兒童總是偏食，只吃肉不吃菜，中國人的國粹⑱
——水餃，就是彌補這方面的不足。大白菜、韭菜⑲、菠菜⑳
……這些兒童排斥的蔬菜，加上豬肉或牛肉就包在水餃裡，無
形中填進了小肚子裡。

　　現在不要以為東方人吃素的多，西方歐美各國也正在風行㉑
「素食主義㉒」呢！因為在東方受佛教的影響，一般有佛教信
仰的民族，都是因具有不殺生的悲憫㉓之心，而不忍心為了口
腹之慾去殺害一條活生生的生命。但是西方的素食者，以另外
角度去衡量素食的利弊㉔。他們除了為了健康的大前提外，還
考慮到「環保」、「污染」、「浪費」……等週邊問題。如飼
養㉕家畜所排泄出的廢物廢氣，及製造肉食工廠所排出的廢水
……直接影響了我們生活的大環境，所以堅決打著「環境保
護」的口號，來倡導㉖素食。尤其因為在健康方面有益，所以
素食能吸引人們加入吃素的行列。如果說素食「有百利而無一
弊」，也不盡然，在成長之中的青少年仍須要大量動物蛋白及
鈣質㉗來強身健骨呢！

一、生詞：New Vocabulary:

1. 素食 sùshí　*N*: vegetarian; vegitarian food

2. 通衢 tōngqú　*N*: thoroughfare; highway

3. 夾雜 jiázá　*V*: to be mingled with; to be mixed up with
   風聲雨聲夾雜著孩子的哭聲使我無法入睡。
   The sounds of wind and rain mingled with the sound of the

child crying made it impossible for me to sleep.

4. 漢堡 hànbǎo　*N:* **hamburger**

5. 披薩 pīsa　*N:* **pizza**

6. 速食店 sùshídiàn　*N:* **fast food restaurant**

7. 盛行 shèngxíng　*V/SV:* **to be popular; to be in vogue**

現在盛行穿名牌的衣服。

It is now in vogue to wear name-brand clothes.

8. 沙拉吧 shālāba　*N:* **salad bar**

9. 啖 dàn　*V:* **to eat; to feed**

現在是冬天，夏天時我要大啖西瓜。

It is now winter; in summer I want to eat a lot of watermelon.

10. 美乃滋 měinǎizī　*N:* **mayonnaise**

11. 攝取 shèqǔ　*V:* **to absorb; to assimilate**

吃橘子可以攝取維他命 C。

Eating oranges one can absorb（more）vitamin C.

12. 維生素 wéishēngsù　*N:* **vitamin**

13. 豆腐 dòufǔ　*N:* **bean curd**

14. 遜於 xùnyú　*V:* **to be inferior to; to be not as good as**

有人說豆漿的營養不遜於牛奶。

Some people say that the nourishment of dou-jiang is as good as（not inferior to）that of milk.

NOTE: dou-jiang is a type of drink made from soy beans which is often drunk at breakfast. It can be found in many flavors and is usually very sweet. Dou-jiang is most commonly translated as "soybean milk" or "soy-milk".

15. 香酥鴨 xiāngsūyā

   N: **crispy duck (a popular Chinese dish made by frying duck meat until crispy)**

16. 炒鱔糊 chǎoshànhú

   N: **fried eel paste (A dish made by frying fresh-water eel)**

17. 穀類 gǔlèi　*N*: **grains; grain-like foods**

18. 國粹 guócuì　*N*: **a unique cultural feature of a nation**

19. 韭菜 jiǔcài　*N*: **leeks; scallions (a type of onion)**

20. 菠菜 bōcài　*N*: **spinach**

21. 風行 fēngxíng　*N*: **to be in fashion; to be popular**

   吃健康食品風行全世界。

   Throughout the world it is in fashion to eat health food.

22. 素食主義 sùshízhǔyì　*N*: **vegetarianism**

23. 悲憫 bēimǐn

   AT: **to have compassion for; to pity; to have sympathy for**

   有些具有悲憫之心的人不願殺生，所以吃素。

   Some compassionate people (people with compassion in their hearts) do not want to kill life (living things), so they eat vegetarian food.

24. 利弊 lìbì

   N: **advantages and disadvantages; pros and cons; gains and losses**

25. 飼養 sìyǎng　*V*: **to raise; to rear**

飼養小動物得有耐心。

Raising small animals requires patience.

26. 倡導 chàngdǎo　*V*: **to propose; to initiate**

這家公司的老闆倡導以微笑服務顧客。

The head of this company proposed (a policy of) serving

customers with a smile.

27. 鈣質 gàizhí　*N*: **calcium content**

二、成語與俗語：Proverbs and Common Sayings:

1. 熙熙攘攘 xīxīrǎngrǎng

crowded and noisy; bustling; coming and going busily

這條街上每天都是熙熙攘攘的。

This street is crowded and noisy (i.e. busy) every day.

2. 各式各樣 gèshìgèyàng

all sorts; all kinds; every variety

她會做各式各樣的蛋糕。

She can make all sorts of cakes.

3. 垂涎三尺 chuíxiánsānchǐ

to yearn for; to drool (over); to covet; to crave

她做的蛋糕使人垂涎三尺。

The cakes which she makes cause people to drool.

4. 花樣百出 huāyàngbǎichū

all kinds; many varieties; many types

現在騙子騙錢的方法花樣百出。

Nowadays swindlers have all kinds of methods for swindling money.

5. 幾可亂真 jīkěluànzhēn

to seem almost genuine; to almost be mistaken for the real thing

壞人印的假鈔票幾可亂真。

The counterfeit money the bad guys printed seemed almost genuine.

6. 色香味俱全 sèxiāngwèijùquán

to be very flavorful; to be very tasty; to smell, look and taste great

媽媽做的菜色香味俱全。

The dishes which mother makes are very flavorful.

7. 大快朵頤 dàkuàiduǒyí

to satisfy the palate

等明天拿到薪水以後，我要到飯館去大快朵頤一番。

Tomorrow, once I get my salary, I want to go to a restaurant and get a meal that will really satisfy my palate.

8. 青菜豆腐保平安 qīngcàidòufǔbǎopíngān

(literally: vegetables and tofu keep things safe and sound)
vegetables and tofu have the vitamins and nutrients necessary for good health

每日三餐不必花很多錢，青菜豆腐保平安。

One should not spend a lot of money for all three meals

...nts necessary for good health.

9. 清_{く一ム}清_{く一ム}淡_{ㄉㄢˋ}淡_{ㄉㄢˋ} qīngqīngdàndàn

light; delicate; simple

夏天太熱，我喜歡吃清清淡淡的食物。

Summer is too hot; I like to eat light foods.

10. 口_{ㄎㄡˇ}腹_{ㄈㄨˋ}之_ㄓ慾_{ㄩˋ} kǒufùzhīyù

to have a great appetite

每天都要滿足口腹之慾的人一定很胖。

People who satisfy their great appetites every day are certain to be fat.

11. 有_{ㄧㄡˇ}百_{ㄅㄞˇ}利_{ㄌㄧˋ}而_{ㄦˊ}無_{ㄨˊ}一_ㄧ弊_{ㄅㄧˋ} yǒubǎiliérwúyíbì

to have many advantages and no disadvantages

吃營養均衡的食物有百利而無一弊。

Eating nutritious, well-balanced foods has many advantages and no disadvantages.

三、句型：Sentence patterns:

1. 不論或……，都會……

no matter X or Y, all can......;

regardless of whether X or Y, both can......

(1) 不論男人或女人都會有自己的愛好。

(2) 不論大城市或小城市都會有書店。

(3) 這個廟不論晴天或雨天都會有人來拜拜。

2. 最……的……可能算是……了

the most ......(thing)......is probably......;

that X which...... most......is probably......

(1) 她最喜歡的花可能算是玫瑰了。

(2) 他最常做的運動可能算是慢跑了。

(3) 動物中和人相處最好的可能算是狗了。

3. ……可代替……

X can be substituted for Y;

X can be used in place of Y

(1) 米飯可代替麵包。

(2) 水果可代替飲料。

(3) 牛奶可代替母奶嗎？

4. ……因具有……而（不）……

because X possesses Y......X can (cannot)......

(1) 他因對這種病具有免疫力，而不會感染。

(2) 人類因具有聰明的頭腦，而能成為萬物的主人。

(3) 鳥類因具有預知天氣變化的能力而能避免受害。

5. 如果說……，也不盡然

If one says......, that doesn't necessarily make it true;

just because one says......does not make it so

(1) 如果說爬山比游泳好，也不盡然。

(2) 如果說春天的風景比秋天的美，也不盡然。

(3) 如果說富人比窮人快樂，也不盡然。

1. 暢快 chàngkuài

   SV: cheerful and exuberant; spiritually elevated; carefree

   這次郊遊正逢天高氣爽，人人都很暢快。

   On this outing the "sky was high and the weather fine" (said of the crisp air in autumn); everyone was cheerful and exuberant.

   愉快 yúkuài　**SV/AT: joyful; pleased; pleasant**

   祝你旅途愉快。

   Wish you a pleasant journey.

   痛快 tòngkuài　**A/SV: delighted; overjoyed**

   喝酒時他很痛快地乾了杯。

   When drinking he delightedly drained the cup.

2. 排斥 páichì

   V/N: to exclude; to expel; to discriminate against; to repel; to reject

   保守的人常排斥新觀念。

   Conservative people often reject new concepts.

   充斥 chōngchì　**V: to flood; to be full of; to be rife with**

   市場上充斥著各式仿冒品。

   The market is flooded with all types of imitations (imitation products).

3. 倡導 chàngdǎo　**V: to initiate; to propose; to promote**

工作人員到鄉下去倡導節育方法。

The workers went to the countryside to promote birth control methods.

提倡 tíchàng　*V*: **to advocate; to encourage**

五四運動是提倡白話文的運動。

The May Fourth Movement advocated the "báihuà" movement.

(NOTE: The May Fourth movement involved a series of student demonstrations held in Peking (now Beijing) on May 4, 1919. Originally held in protest of the government's surrender to the Twenty-One Demands from Japan, the demonstrations touched off a series of critical reforms. One of the most important of these was the introduction of "báihuà" into the literary mainstream. "Báihuà" was the use of vernacular (spoken) language in the written form. Prior to its introduction, written Chinese used a stylized form which bore little resemblance to spoken Chinese.)

4. 吸引 xīyǐn　*V*: **to attract; to draw**

速食店吸引了不少顧客。

Fast food restaurants attract many customers.

引誘 yǐnyòu　*V*: **to lure; to seduce**

壞朋友常引誘年輕人誤入歧途。

Bad friends often lure young people onto the wrong path (in

life).

5. 忍ㄖㄣˇ心ㄒㄧㄣ rěnxīn

A/V: to have the heart to; to be hardhearted enough to

看過的好書常不忍心丟掉。

After reading through a good book (I) often do not have the heart to throw it away.

耐ㄋㄞˋ心ㄒㄧㄣ nàixīn **N: patience**

與兒童相處一定得有耐心。

Getting along with children definitely requires patience.

五、問題討論：Questions for Discussion:

1. 速食的種類有哪些？

_____

2. 如果你想請人吃飯時應注意什麼？

_____

3. 如果小孩偏食應該怎麼辦？

_____

4. 你喜歡吃什麼素菜？

_____

5. 為什麼中國素菜飯館的菜做得像雞、鴨、魚、肉一樣？

_____

6. 肉類對環境有什麼影響？

_____

六、練習：Practice Exercises:

1. 選擇相似詞：（其中有複選）

Select the Word or Phrase with the Same Meaning:

(1) 佐料： ____　　*a.*調味料　　*b.*資料　　*c.*料理

(2) 以及： ____　　*a.*和　　　　*b.*跟　　　*c.*與

(3) 料到： ____　　*a.*材料　　　*b.*想到　　*c.*猜到

(4) 風行： ____　　*a.*流行　　　*b.*實行　　*c.*行列

(5) 利弊： ____　　*a.*錢幣　　　*b.*好壞　　*c.*優劣

2. 填空：

Fill in the Blanks:

(1) 各式各樣的蔬菜擺滿一桌，令人 _____ 三尺。

(2) 以豆腐皮炸出的香酥鴨，吃起來幾可 _____

(3) 中國人一向說：青菜 _____ 保平安。

(4) 不忍心為了 _____ 之慾，去殺害一條活生生的生命。

(5) 西方的素食者以另外一個角度去 _____ 素食的利弊。

(6) 如果說素食有 _____ 而無一害，也不盡然。

3. 造句：

Make Sentences:

(1) 夾雜： _____

(2) 豐富： _____

(3) 遜於： _____

(4) 無形中： _____

(5) 飼養： _____

(6) 花樣百出：_____

(7) 大快朵頤：_____

(8) 不論……或……都會……：_____

佳文欣賞

落花生

許地山

　　我們屋後有半畝隙地。母親說：「讓他荒蕪著怪可惜，既然你們那麼愛吃花生，就闢來做花生園罷。」我們幾姊弟和幾個小丫頭都很喜歡——買種的買種，動土的動土，灌園的灌園；過不了幾個月，居然收穫了！

　　媽媽說：「今晚我們可以做一個收穫節，也請你們的爹爹來嘗嘗我們的新花生，如何？」我們都答應了。母親把花生做成好幾樣的食品，還吩咐這節期要在園裡的茅亭舉行。

　　那晚上的天色不大好，可是爹爹也到來，實在很難得！爹爹說：「你們愛吃花生麼？」

　　我們都爭著答應：「愛！」

　　「誰能把花生的好處說出來？」

　　姊姊說：「花生的氣味很美。」

　　哥哥說：「花生可以製油。」

　　我說：「無論何等人都可以用賤價買他來吃；都喜歡吃

他。這就是他的好處。」

　　爹爹說：「花生的用處固然很多；但有一樣是很可貴的。這小小的豆不像那好看的蘋果、桃子、石榴，把他們的果實懸在枝上，鮮紅嫩綠的顏色，令人一望而發生羨慕的心。他只把果子埋在地底，等到成熟，才容人把他挖出來，你們偶然看見一棵花生瑟縮地長在地上，不能立刻辨出他有沒有果實，非得等到你接觸他才能知道。」

　　我們都說：「是的。」母親也點點頭。爹爹接下去說：「所以你們要像花生，因為他是有用的，不是偉大、好看的東西。」我說：「那麼，人要做有用的人，不要做偉大、體面的人了。」爹爹說：「這是我對於你們的希望。」

　　我們談到夜闌才散。所有花生食品雖然沒有了，然而父親的話現在還印在我心版上。

第十三課　李天祿①的掌中戲②和茶藝

　　八十二歲的李天祿，從十四歲和掌中戲結緣③，就一直執著④於這份民俗技藝⑤。幾十年下來不僅演遍大江南北，贏得⑥掌聲⑦，同時遠赴歐美巡迴⑧公演，教外國人看掌中戲，學掌中戲。另外，他還迷戀⑨著一分茶香。

　　「我不喝茶，就吃不下飯！」李天祿一邊幫學生倒茶，一邊說。

　　茶藝⑩是時髦⑪的標籤⑫。除了燙壺⑬、溫杯⑭、注水⑮等動作外，還得注意傳統喝茶裡的禮數。李天祿認為將茶水浸⑯久一些較能泡⑰出味道，所以晚些倒茶給客人成為一種尊重，先倒茶給自己則象徵謙遜⑱。

　　李天祿喝茶沒有「亦宛然⑲」戲團雕樑畫棟的舞臺，有的只是一把不銹鋼⑳的水壺、宜興㉑壺加上鶯歌㉒燒製的茶杯而已。他認為好茶入喉，滑溜㉓像茶油，入口就化，感覺嘴巴像沒喝到茶就直奔喉嚨㉔，但不久回味無窮，兩頰生津。李天祿的茶齡㉕和演戲同壽㉖，二十二歲自組「亦宛然」開始，平均一年三百臺戲，每場都必攜茶為伴。

　　李天祿的許多學生裡，有大學生、有外國人，他們除了學演掌中戲，就是學品茗㉗。「喝茶，卻很少買茶！」不是茶農送茶，就是戲迷贈茶，或是仰慕㉘者禮茶，雖然茶的種類繁多㉙，李天祿最中意㉚的是武夷茶㉛。有出國機會，他就找茶，買回好茶，與戲班、好友一同分享㉜。

　　他控制著手中的木偶，傳神㉝地演出悲歡離合，人情世事，自己也成了戲中人。喝茶對他來說不是雅事㉞，而是生活裡必不可缺的事。

　　他得知唐朝㉟陸羽㊱寫茶經㊲，大談喝茶之道後，有興趣以陸羽為故事，編寫㊳一齣㊴陸羽的木偶戲㊵。他一邊構思，一邊興奮地發現木偶的握茶、品茶可以栩栩如生。相信以他六十多年的茶齡和掌中戲演出經驗，以陸羽為題的掌中戲，必定很值得看。

〜節錄自〈茶戲人生〉《行遍天下雜誌》〜

一、生詞： New Vocabulary:

1. 李ㄌㄧˇ天ㄊㄧㄢ祿ㄌㄨˋ LiTiānlù　**PN:** 木偶戲大師

　the name of a famous master puppeteer

2. 掌ㄓㄤˇ中ㄓㄨㄥ戲ㄒㄧˋ zhǎngzhōngxì　**PN:** 用手操縱人物表演的戲

　a hand-puppet performance; a puppet show

3. 結ㄐㄧㄝˊ緣ㄩㄢˊ jiéyuán

　VO: to form a connection or bond; to associate on good terms; to have a bond or connection

她從小就跟花結了緣。

She, since childhood, has had a bond with flowers.

4. 執著 zhízhuó

V: to be committed (e.g. to a cause, an issue, etc.)

這個學生執著於師生之禮。

This student is committed to (the customary) etiquette between students and their teachers.

5. 民俗技藝 mínsújìyì　**N: 各民族傳統的表現技能的藝術**

arts or crafts unique to a certain people or nation

6. 贏得 yíngdé　**V: to win; to gain**

我們學校的籃球隊贏得了冠軍。

Our school's basketball team won the championship.

7. 掌聲 zhǎngshēng　**N: clapping; applause**

8. 巡迴 xúnhuí

V/AT: to circulate; to make rounds; to make a circuit of; to tour around

這個合唱團要到全國各地巡迴表演。

This chorus will tour around (every place in) the country performing.

9. 迷戀 míliàn　**V: to be infatuated with; to indulge in**

孩子們不要迷戀電動玩具而忘了念書。

Children should not get infatuated with video games and forget to study.

10. 茶藝 cháyì　**N: the art of preparing tea**

11. 時髦 shímáo

SV/AT: (a) to be stylish, fashionable; to be in vogue

(b) stylish, fashionable

(*a*) 她穿的衣服很時髦。

The clothes she wears are very stylish.

(*b*) 這是一種時髦的行業。

This is a very fashionable occupation.

12. 標籤 biāoqiān　**N: a label; a tag**

13. 燙壺 tànghú　**VO: to heat a (tea) pot**

泡茶以前先要燙壺。

Before steeping tea one should heat the pot.

14. 溫杯 wēnbēi　**VO: to warm the (tea) cup**

燙壺以後再溫杯。

After heating the pot one then warms the (tea) cups.

15. 注水 zhùshuǐ　**VO: to pour water**

泡茶時要注入滾水。

When it is time to steep the tea one should pour in boiling water.

16. 浸 jìn　**V: to steep; to soak**

把衣服浸在肥皂水裡一小時以後再洗，會洗得比較乾淨。

Letting clothes soak in soapy water for an hour and then washing them again can make them much cleaner.

17. 泡 pào　**V: to steep (tea); to soak**

把洗乾淨的青菜泡在又鹹又辣的水裡可做成泡菜。

Green vegetables which have been washed clean can be steeped in salty, spicy water to make pickled vegetables.

18. 謙遜 qiānxùn　*SV/AT*: **to be modest and unassuming**

他的態度總是那麼謙遜。

His manner is always so modest and unassuming.

19. 亦宛然 yìwǎnrán　*PN*: 木偶戲班

the name of a puppet theater troupe

20. 不銹鋼 búxiùgāng

N: **stainless steel (non-rusting steel)**

21. 宜興 yáxīng　*PN*: 江蘇省地名以出產茶壺有名

a county in Jiang Su province famous for its tea pots

22. 鶯歌 yīnggē　*PN*: 臺灣省地名著名的陶瓷產地

a village in Taiwan famous for its pottery

23. 滑溜 huáliū　*SV/AT*: **to be smooth; to be slippery**

地太滑溜，走路要小心，以免滑倒。

The ground is too slippery; walk carefully and avoid slipping and falling.

24. 喉嚨 hóulóng　*N*: **throat**

25. 茶齡 chálíng

N: **length of time spent acquainting oneself with tea (often said in regard to the practice of a tea expert)**

26. 壽 shòu　*N*: **period of time within one's lifetime**

27. 品茗 pǐnmíng

VO: **to drink tea with critical appreciation of its taste and**

quality; to savor a cup of good tea

爸爸每天晚飯後都要品茗。

Every day after the evening meal, father always wants to savor a cup of good tea.

28. 仰慕 yǎngmù

V: **to hold somebody in high esteem; to greatly respect someone**

我仰慕那些有學問仍不斷努力研究的人。

I hold in high esteem those people who are knowledgeable and still unceasingly exert themselves in research.

29. 繁多 fánduō

AT: **to be numerous; to be many; to be manifold**

天上繁多的星星，數不清。

The stars in the sky are numerous; they are countless (too numerous to count).

30. 中意 zhòngyì

V: **to be to one's liking; to be to one's preference**

這家鞋店的鞋子，你有中意的嗎？

Does this shoe store have any shoes which are to your liking?

31. 武夷茶 wǔyíchá　*PN*: 福建武夷山出產的茶

a special tea harvested from Wu Yi mountain in Fu Jian province

32. 分享 fēnxiǎng　*V*: **to share**

我做了一個大蛋糕請朋友分享。

I made a big cake and invited my friends to share it.

33. 傳神 chuánshén　*SV*: **to be vivid; to be life-like**

他雕刻的人或動物都很傳神。

The people and animals which he carves are all very life-like.

34. 雅事 yǎshì　*N*: **the refined activities of the intelligentsia**

35. 唐朝 Tángcháo　*PN*: 中國的朝代名

China's Tang Dynasty (618 A.D. - 907 A.D.)

36. 陸羽 Lùyǔ　*N*:《茶經》一書的作者

the "tea-maniac" (茶顛), a Tang dynasty man-of-letters who was so fond of tea that he wrote the book 茶經.

37. 茶經 Chájīng　*PN*: 書名, 陸羽所著

A book written by 陸羽 during the Tang Dynasty.

The book touches on every aspect of tea drinking; including not only how to choose good teas, but also how to go about preparing and drinking them.

38. 編寫 biānxiě　*V*: **to compile**

李教授打算編寫一部地名大詞典。

Professor Li plans to compile a dictionary of place names.

39. 齣 chū　*M*: **measure word for (stage) plays**

這個戲院每天演三齣戲。

This theater shows three plays every day.

40. 木偶戲 mùǒuxì　*PN*: 戲劇的一種 (同掌中戲)

a hand-puppet performance; a puppet show

二、成語與俗語： Proverbs and Common Sayings:

1. 大江南北 dàjiāngnánběi

   (literally: both sides of the Yangtse River - the dividing line between North and South China); throughout a vast area

   大江南北的風景、氣候都不一樣。

   The scenery and climate on either side of the Yangtse River is not at all the same.

2. 雕樑畫棟 diāoliánghuàdòng

   (literally: carved beams and painted rafters) an ornate building

   如果住在雕樑畫棟的屋子裡，你有什麼感覺？

   How would you feel if you lived in an ornate house (a house with carved beams and painted rafters)?

3. 入口就化 rùkǒujiùhuà

   to melt in your mouth

   冰淇淋入口就化。

   Ice cream melts in your mouth.

4. 回味無窮 húiwèiwúqióng

   to endlessly enjoy in retrospect; to ponder and savor over and over again ; unforgettable

   看了這部電影使我回味無窮。

   Having seen that movie, I endlessly enjoy it in retrospect.

5. 兩頰生津 liǎngjiáshēngjīn

to be mouth watering; to whet one's appetite

吃了她做的菜使大家兩頰生津。

Eating the dishes she made causes everyone's mouth to water.

6. 悲歡離合 bēihuānlíhé

the sorrows of partings and the joys of reunions which life has to offer; the varied (and often bitter) experiences which life has to offer

古今中外的戲劇都是表現悲歡離合的。

Theater throughout time and from every place has been an expression of the varied experiences which life has to offer.

7. 人情世事 rénqíngshìshì

human feelings, sympathies and the affairs of human life; the ways of the world; the ways of human beings and society

小孩子不懂人情世事。

Small children do not understand the ways of the world.

8. 栩栩如生 xǔxǔrúshēng

to be life-like; to be true-to-life

他畫的老虎栩栩如生。

The tigers which he paints are life-like.

三、句型：Sentence Patterns:

1. 從……就一直……

......since......has always (continued to)......;

......from......continues to......

(1) 他從小就一直喜歡爬山。

(2) 總統每天從早就一直忙到晚。

(3) 他從晚上十點到天亮就一直沒睡著覺。

2. 除了……還得……

......besides......still must......;

......in addition to......also must......

(1) 今年我除了戒煙還得戒酒。

(2) 每天她除了上班還得做飯。

(3) 這個小女孩每天除了學唱歌還得學跳舞。

3. ……沒有……，有的只是……

......has no......all that can be found is......;

......does not have......all that there is, is......

(1) 這個山上沒有人，有的只是一群一群的羊。

(2) 窮人的家裡沒有好看的家具，有的只是破桌椅而已。

(3) 這裡沒有大河，有的只是小溪而已。

4. ……對……來說，不是……而是……

in regards to X, is not...but is actually......;

in the case of X, (the case) is not......but in fact is......

(1) 教書對他來說不是苦而是樂。

(2) 對中年人來說，營養過多不是有益而是有害。

(3) 孩子太多對一個家庭來說不是樂而是苦。

四、易混淆的詞：Easily Confused Words:

1. 執著 zhízhuó　　*V: to maintain; to uphold*

他執著於自己的原則，從不接受別人的建議。

He upholds his own personal principles; he never accepts other people's advice.

固ㄍㄨˋ執ㄓˊ gùzhí　*SV/V*: **to be stubborn; to be obstinate**

他很固執，不輕易更改生活上的習慣。

He is very obstinate; it is not easy (for him) to change the habits of a lifetime.

頑ㄨㄢˊ固ㄍㄨˋ wángù

SV: **to be very conservative; to be ultra-conservative**

老人多半很頑固，不喜歡新的式樣。

Most old people are very conservative; they do not like new styles.

2. 迷ㄇㄧˊ戀ㄌㄧㄢˋ míliàn

V: **to be infatuated with; to be in blind love with**

我們迷戀海邊的落日，真捨不得離開。

We are infatuated with seaside sunsets and dislike being separated from them.

迷ㄇㄧˊ上ㄕㄤˋ míshàng　*V*: **to be fascinated by**

小孩子迷上了拼圖遊戲，越拼越有經驗。

Children are fascinated by puzzles; the more they put together the more experienced they become.

著ㄓㄠˊ迷ㄇㄧˊ zháomí

SV: **to become absorbed by; to be caught up in**

武俠小說令人著迷，有人看得廢寢忘食。

People can become absorbed in reading novels depicting the chivalry and prowess of ancient Chinese swordsmen; some people can become so absorbed in them that they forget to eat or sleep.

沉迷 chénmí **V: to be addicted to; to be hooked on**

他沉迷賭博，以致家破人亡。

He is addicted to gambling; consequently, his home is in ruins and his family is scattered.

3. 時髦 shímáo *SV/AT*: **to be fashionable; to be in vogue**

她剪了一頭時髦的短髮。

She cut her hair in a short and very fashionable style.

流行 liúxíng *V/SV*: **to be prevalent; to be popular**

現在流行短髮。現在短髮很流行。

Nowadays short hair is prevalent. Nowadays short hair is very popular.

摩登 módēng *SV/AT*: **to be modern; to be fashionable**

他家的家具十分摩登，都是現代化式樣。

The furniture in his home is completely modern; it is all of a modern style.

4. 禮數 lǐshù

N: different grades of courtesy based on differences in one's rank

禮數是在什麼樣的情形，有什麼樣的禮貌。

"禮數" means appropriate manners under different circumstances.

禮貌 lǐmaò　　*N*: **etiquette; good manners; decorum**

有禮貌的人是以誠懇的態度尊重別人。

People with good manners respect other people through a sincere attitude.

禮節 lǐjié

N: **the rules of politeness; the requirements of decorum**

中國人接待客人應有的禮節越來越簡化了。

The rules of decorum by which the Chinese receive guests are becoming more and more simplified.

5. 象徵 xiàngzhēng　　*V*: **to symbolize; to signify**

綠色象徵和平，白色象徵純潔。

(The color) green symbolizes peace, (the color) white signifies purity.

代表 dàibiǎo　　*V/N*: **to represent; to stand for**

他代表國家出席國際會議。

He represented his country at the international conference.

6. 謙遜 qiānxùn　　*N*: **a modest and unassuming nature**

謙遜的人有禮讓的態度。

People with a modest and unassuming nature have a manner which gives precedence to others out of courtesy or thoughtfulness.

謙虛 qiānxū　　*SV*: **to be modest; to be self-effacing**

他很謙虛，虛心而不自大。

He is very modest; he is open-minded and not arrogant.

虛ㄒㄩ偽ㄨㄟˋ xūwèi

SV: to be hypocritical; to be false; to be insincere

虛偽的人不算謙虛，而是不實在。

Insincere people should not be regarded as self-effacing, but rather as dishonest.

五、問題討論：Questions for Discussion:

1. 你看過木偶戲嗎？是怎樣表演的？

_____

2. 李天祿到過什麼地方表演木偶戲？

_____

3. 他除了喜歡木偶戲，還迷戀著什麼？

_____

4. 為什麼李天祿很少買茶？

_____

5. 他的學生裡有些什麼人？跟他學什麼？

_____

6. 陸羽是什麼朝代的人？寫過一部什麼書？

_____

六、練習：Practice Exercises:

1. 選擇相反詞：

Select the Word or Phrase with the Opposite Meaning:

(1) 時髦：　____　 *a.*過時　 *b.*流行　 *c.*現代

⑵ 尊重：___　　*a.*尊敬　*b.*鄙視　*c.*輕微

⑶ 謙遜：___　　*a.*傲慢　*b.*謙虛　*c.*順從

⑷ 繁多：___　　*a.*稀少　*b.*奇異　*c.*減少

⑸ 分享：___　　*a.*共享　*b.*享有　*c.*獨享

⑹ 雅事：___　　*a.*文雅　*b.*俗事　*c.*粗俗

⑺ 興奮：___　　*a.*頹喪　*b.*後悔　*c.*高興

2.選擇同音字：

Select the Character with the Same Pronunciation:

⑴ 赴：___　　*a.*富　*b.*卜　*c.*趕

⑵ 籤：___　　*a.*兼　*b.*廉　*c.*千

⑶ 浸：___　　*a.*侵　*b.*進　*c.*淨

⑷ 亦：___　　*a.*也　*b.*意　*c.*夷

⑸ 齣：___　　*a.*出　*b.*句　*c.*處

⑹ 栩：___　　*a.*羽　*b.*取　*c.*許

⑺ 攜：___　　*a.*溪　*b.*期　*c.*摧

⑻ 銹：___　　*a.*透　*b.*誘　*c.*秀

⑼ 仰：___　　*a.*迎　*b.*昂　*c.*養

⑽ 遜：___　　*a.*訓　*b.*孫　*c.*順

3.填空：

Fill in the Blanks:

⑴ 李天祿從十四歲和____戲____，就一直____於這份民俗
　　___。

⑵ 茶藝除了__壺、__杯、__水等動作外，還得注意傳統喝茶的
　　___。

⑶ 他認為好茶入喉，____像茶油，入口就__。

(4) 他喝茶沒有＿＿＿畫棟的舞臺，只有一把不＿＿水壺和鶯歌＿＿＿製的茶杯而已。

(5) 他控＿著手中的木偶，傳神的演出悲歡＿＿＿。

(6) 他興奮地發現木偶的握茶、品茶可以＿＿＿如生。

第十四課 電子字典

　　輕薄短小、方便攜帶的電子字典[1]，從三年前問世[2]以來，部分教育界人士對這種新型電子產品採保留[3]態度，但它卻很受在職人士和學生歡迎。不過電子字典能否使人類從「翻字典」轉入「按字典」的時代，仍須要考驗。

　　市場競爭使得電子產品不斷地推陳出新。有萊思康、無敵等幾種牌子。從簡單的英漢字典發展到現在已具有的漢英、同義字[4]、繁簡字體[5]、發音、多國旅遊會話、拼音校正、英文測驗和醫藥、汽車的專業字典等多種功能。有的字典還包括了約會、記事、電話名片、定時鬧鐘、計算機，以及顯示時差[6]、貨幣[7]、度量衡[8]和陰陽曆等的換算[9]功能。

　　電子字典攜帶方便、反應敏捷[10]。這種新產品帶來了新鮮感，同時帶起學習外語的熱潮[11]，達到教育的目的。但是由於內容過於簡化，對學英文的人有誤導[12]的危險。其效用僅限於幫助學生背單字或增加字彙，對真正學英文的人幫助不大。因此目前並未威脅[13]到傳統印刷字典的市場。

　　電子字典在不同的市場，也遇到不同語文的問題。按普通話發音的注音或漢語拼音簡易輸入法，就對香港粵語[14]使用者

造成困擾⑮。

　　在購買前，先認清自己的須要再去購買。另外要測試⑯何種字數量最多，例如設定一段字母由 th 到 ti 之間，就可以測出哪個機種所包涵的字最多。同時想瞭解這個字典是否跟得上時代，只要輸入酸雨⑰、關稅及貿易總協定⑱、愛滋病⑲等常用的新聞字，就可知道是否是老版本⑳的字典。

　　隨著時代和科技的進步，電子字典已成為不少人隨身攜帶的字典了。

一、生詞：New Vocabulary:

1. 電子字典 diànzǐzìdiǎn　　*N*: electronic dictionary

2. 問世 wènshì

V: to come out;　to be released for public use for the first time; to be published for the first time; to be released to the market

這部新發明的機器何時問世？

When will this newly invented machine be released to the market?

3. 保留 bǎuliú　　*V*: retain

好的習慣應保留，壞的習慣應革除。

Good habits should be retained; bad habits should be gotten rid of.

4. 同義字 tóngyìzì　　*N*: synonym

5. 繁簡字體 fánjiǎnzìtǐ

   N: complex and simplified Chinese characters (as a combined set)

6. 時差 shíchā

   N: time difference (between different regions or countries)

7. 貨幣 huòbì　**N: money; currency**

8. 度量衡 dùlínghéng　**N: weights and measures**

9. 換算 huànsuàn　**V: to convert; conversion**

   一美元換算成臺幣是多少？

   One American Dollar converts to how many Taiwanese NT dollars?

10. 敏捷 mǐnjié　**SV: to be agile; to be quick; to be nimble**

    獵人的動作很敏捷。

    Hunters' movements are very agile.

11. 熱潮 rècháo

    N: a popular fad; a practice which is in vogue

12. 誤導 wùdǎo　**V: to be a bad influence; to mislead**

    模特兒的身材，常常誤導年輕女孩子吃得太少。

    The figures of models often mislead young women to eat too little.

13. 威脅 wēixié

    V/N: to threaten; to imperil; to menace; to intimidate

    父母希望孩子的功課好，用威脅的方法是不對的。

    Parents hope that their children's schoolwork is good; using intimidation (however) is wrong.

14. 粵語 yuèyǔ

  N: Cantonese, the language of Canton province

15. 困擾 kùnrǎo

  V/SV/N: to trouble one (i.e. a problem, a puzzle); to worry

  one; to bother one

  這件事一直困擾著我。

  This business has really been troubling me.

16. 測試 cèshì　　**V: to try out; to test out; to experiment with**

  一部新機器一定要經過測試才能用。

  A new machine should be tried out before it can be used.

17. 酸雨 suānyǔ　　**N: acid rain**

18. 關稅及貿易總協定 guānshuìjímàoyìzǒngxiédìng

  N: GATT, The General / Agreement on Tariffs and Trade

19. 愛滋病 aìzībìng

  N: A.I.D.S., Acquired Immune Deficiency Syndrome

20. 老版本 lǎobǎnběn

  N: an original literary work; an original manuscript; an

  old edition

二、成語與俗語：Proverbs and Common Sayings:

1. 推陳出新 tuīchénchūxīn

  to weed through the old in search of the new; to find new

  ways of doing things using old theories; to find something

new in what is old; to improve upon something

電器的產品，不斷地推陳出新。

Electronic products are continuously being improved upon.

三、句型： Sentence Patterns:

1. ……能否……仍須要……

……can or can not……still must……;

……able to or not……still has to……

⑴ 他的病能否治好，仍須要觀察。

⑵ 他能否考上有名的大學，仍須要努力。

⑶ 交通問題能否解決，仍須要研究。

2. 由於……過於……，對……有……

owing to……exceeds……, this is having the effect that…has……;

as the result of…… is extremely……, the result is…… has become……

⑴ 由於今年冬天天氣過於寒冷，對農作物有害。

⑵ 由於他的工作過於勞累，對他的健康有損。

⑶ 最近由於經濟過於不景氣，對工商業有很大的影響。

3. 只要……就可……

(one) just needs to……then (one) can……;

once one……then one is able to……

⑴ 只要到十八歲就可以當兵。

⑵ 只要問查號臺，就可知道你要的電話號碼。

⑶ 只要爬上這個山頂，就可欣賞美麗的風景。

四、易混淆的詞： Easily Confused Words:

1. 具有 jùyǒu　***V*: to have; to be provided with; to possess**

發明家具有超人的智力。

Inventors possess a super-human intelligence.

擁有 yǒngyǒu　***V*: to own**

地主擁有農地。

The landlord owns farmland.

懷有 huáiyǒu　***V*: to harbor; to yearn for; to embrace**

慈母懷有愛兒女的心。

A loving mother has a heart (capable of) yearning for her children.

2. 功能 gōngnéng

***N*: a function (of a system, etc.); an effect; a use**

多種功能的電腦較受歡迎。

Computers with many functions are in greater demand (receive a greater welcome).

性能 xìngnéng

***N*: a property; the function (of a machine, etc.)**

工程師一定要了解各式機械的性能。

Engineers definitely understand every type of mechanical function.

才能 cáinéng　***N*: an ability; a talent**

個人的才能，在工作上可以表現出來。

An individual's talent can be manifested in their work.

3. 困擾 kùnrǎo

V/N: to worry one; to be troublesome to one

能克服困擾的人，一定成功。

People who can overcome difficulties will definitely succeed.

干擾 gānrǎo **V/N: to harry; to interfere; to intervene**

外行人不能干擾內行人做的事。

Nonprofessional people should not interfere with the work of professionals.

打擾 dǎrǎo **V/N: to disturb**

在圖書館不可大聲談笑，以免打擾別人。

In order to avoid disturbing other people in the library one should not talk or laugh loudly.

4. 包含 bāohán **V: to embody; to imply; to contain**

有些詞彙包含很多意思，不可亂用。

Some words (vocabulary items) contain many meanings, one cannot use them too sloppily.

包括 bāokùo

V: to consist of; to include; to comprise of

秘書工作除了安排開會，整理資料，還包括接電話。

Secretarial work, in addition to arranging meetings and organizing information, also includes answering the telephones.

5. 反ㄈㄢˇ應ㄧㄥˋ fǎnyìng　*V/N*: **to react; to respond; a reaction**

學生的反應可以顯示教材是否合適。

Student reactions can demonstrate whether teaching materials are appropriate.

反ㄈㄢˇ映ㄧㄥˋ fǎnyìng

V/N: **to depict; to portray; to mirror; a reflection**

有些問題常常反映出相關的問題。

Certain problems often indicate (reflect) related problems.

反ㄈㄢˇ射ㄕㄜˋ fǎnshè

V/N: **to bounce light back; to reflect ; reflex action**

太陽光從水面上反射到樹林中。

The sunlight reflected from the surface of the water into the forest.

五、問題討論： Questions for Discussion:

1. 電子字典的優缺點。

---

2. 電子字典為何不斷的推陳出新？

---

3. 請舉出電子字典的七種功能。

---

4. 如何才能知道這個電子字典能否跟得上時代？

---

5. 電子字典對學英文有什麼好處或壞處？

六、練習 : Practice Exercises:

1. 選相似詞：（其中有複選）

Select the Word or Phrase with the Same Meaning:

(1) 在職人士： ___   *a.*上班族   *b.*賦閒人士   *c.*有職業的人

(2) 競爭： ___   *a.*戰爭   *b.*競賽   *c.*比賽

(3) 校正： ___   *a.*改正   *b.*更正   *c.*學校

(4) 包括： ___   *a.*包含   *b.*內容   *c.*包圍

(5) 威脅： ___   *a.*脅迫   *b.*威風   *c.*威力

(6) 敏捷： ___   *a.*快速   *b.*迅速   *c.*聰敏

(7) 過於： ___   *a.*過分   *b.*經過   *c.*太

(8) 粵語： ___   *a.*上海話   *b.*廣東話   *c.*閩南話

2. 造句：

Make Sentences:

(1) 採……態度： _____

(2) 能否： _____

(3) 校正： _____

(4) 顯示： _____

(5) 敏捷： _____

(6) 威脅： _____

(7) 僅限於： _____

(8) 隨身： _____

(9) 測試： _____

3.配句：

Match the Correct Sentence Fragments:

(1) 電子字典（　）

(2) 市場產品競爭大（　）

(3) 漢英字典（　）

(4) 普通話發音的字典（　）

(5) 長途旅行的人（　）

(6) 英文字典內容過於簡化（　）

(7) 計算機（　）

(8) 人類將從「翻字典」（　）

(9) 電子字典的牌子（　）

(10) 近來常用的新聞字有（　）

a. 有漢英發音、拼音、校正等功能

b. 有時會有時差的困擾

c. 可以幫助我們做度量衡的換算

d. 攜帶方便，反應敏捷，輕薄短小

e. 對學英文的人有誤導的危險

f. 有萊思康、無敵等

g. 應不斷地推陳出新

h. 酸雨、愛滋病等

i. 轉入「按字典」的時代

j. 使香港粵語使用者造成困擾

閱讀與探討
Read and Discuss

全方位通訊系統

——工具書——字典及辭典的使用——

農人種田，須要使用犁、鋤等工具；工人製作器物，須要使用鋸、

斧等工具；我們讀書求學問，也須要使用工具； 這些工具，我們稱為
工具書。所謂工具書，是搜集許多資料，按照一定的方法，加以編排，
使我們可以從裡面找到所須要的答案的書籍。它可以解答我們的疑難，
糾正我們的錯誤，增進我們的了解，對我們有很大的幫助。

　　工具書的範圍很廣，其中我們最常使用的就是字典和辭典。字典
可以告訴我們單字的正確寫法 (形)、讀 音(音) 和意義 (義)；辭典可以
告訴我們許多辭語，包括人名、地名、制度、成語、典故……等的含
義。一般的字典，除了解釋單字以外，往往也解釋由兩個或兩個以上
的單字所組成的詞語；普通的辭典都是把搜集到的詞語，編排在詞語
的第一個單字下面；所以字典往往具有辭典的功用，而辭典也往往具
有字典的功用。因此，我們每個人，至少應該準備一本字典或辭典，
隨時查用。

　　要使用字典及辭典，必須知道字典、辭典的編排方式。一般字典、
辭典的編排方式，可分成二類：

1.按注音符號順序編排的方式

　　　使用這一類的字典或辭典，只要確定要查的字的讀音然後按照
讀音，便可查到這個字了。

　　　凡是按注音符號順序編排的字典、辭典，多半附有部首和筆畫
順序的檢字表，如果遇到不能確定讀音的字，可以去翻查檢字表。

2.按部首編排的方式

　　　使用這一類的字典、辭典，首先必須確定要查的單字或詞語第
一個字的部首；找到部首以後，再把這個字扣除部首以外的筆畫算
清楚；最後按照筆畫數目，便可以查到這個單字，或在這個單字下
面查到要找的詞語了。

　　　凡是按部首編排的字典、辭典，多半附有難檢字的筆畫檢字表，
如果遇到不能確定部首的字，可以翻查檢字表。

　　查到了自己所要找的字或詞語以後，要特別注意的是，大多數的字或詞語，往往有好幾個不同的解釋，所以還必須根據文章的上下文，把最適當的解釋挑選出來，才不會造成錯誤。

　　除了一般所使用的普通辭典以外，還有專門性的辭典，例如有關人名、地名、動物、植物、地質、礦物、教育、文學、成語……等，都各有專門辭典。如果我們遇到比較專門的詞語，在普通辭典裡查不到，就要去查考專門辭典了。各種辭典都有它的使用方法，只要參看它們的例言或說明，便知道怎樣去使用了。

——國中《國文》第一冊〈語文常識〉。國立編譯館——

第十五課　消費市場的新客

　　由於以成人為主的消費市場漸趨飽和①，青少年「有錢有閒」的消費潛力②，近來吸引更多業者投入青少年市場的開發，這股風潮直接衝擊③國內九〇年代的消費結構④。

　　一份長期暢銷⑤的《青少年週刊⑥》負責人說：「一個禮拜可以賣掉五萬本，幾乎是零庫存⑦。」出版界原來擔心現在年輕人不愛看書的習慣，會導致⑧國內市場萎縮⑨，但青少年在多元化⑩社會中培養出來的新興趣，反而促使出版市場有更多元化的發展。

　　雖然一般青少年沒有收入，但隨著父母的薪水年年增加，青少年的零用金也相對⑪增加。另外，不少青年學生以打工⑫賺取外快⑬，都使青少年市場的潛力不可忽視⑭。

　　出版界人士表示，迎合⑮青少年的出版品，多以娛樂性、輕鬆性的「商品」居多，因此，一本書字數不必太多，反而賣得好。另一方面，為因應⑯青少年可觀⑰的消費實力，不但傳統書店的商品結構中大量增加最容易讓青少年掏腰包⑱購買的言情小說⑲、服裝、飾品雜誌、漫畫書⑳和小書卡㉑，甚至有以專賣店型態出現的「漫畫屋」(其中最紅的漫畫人物是加菲貓

GARFIELD)㉒，在學生商圈中，如雨後春筍般的成立。不管有聲或無聲的出版品，都不忘抓住青少年這群市場上的新財主。

　　以青少年作為主要客人，除了百貨公司的文具、禮品、運動品等專櫃㉓、超級商店、速食店之外，MTV、KTV、酒吧以及柏青哥㉔，都是青少年喜歡流連㉕的地方。這些行業因它們的到來，所以生意興隆。

　　現在小孩也和大人一樣，品牌㉖意識力㉗很強，例如：一位國中學生喜歡 FIDO DIDO 的產品㉘，高中生指名㉙要買千元以上的名牌鋼筆 CROSS 等高單價的商品，出手闊綽㉚，而且不像大人偶而㉛會討價還價，對業者來說，實在是很好的顧客。

一、生詞：New Vocabulary:

1. 飽和 bǎohé　*V: to saturate; saturation; saturated*

   這個城市的人口已經飽和了。

   The population of this city has already reached saturation.

2. 潛力 qiánlì　**N: potential; latent capacity; potentiality**

3. 衝擊 chōngjí

   V/N: **to lash; to pound against; to strike against; to deal a blow to**

   進口的產品太多，衝擊著本國的工業。

   There are too many imported products; it is dealing a blow to domestic industries.

4. 結構 jiégòu　**N: structure; construction; composition**

5. 暢銷 chàngxiāo

SV/AT: **to sell like hotcakes; to sell really well**

今年哪一部小說最暢銷？

Which was the best selling novel this year?

6. 週刊 zhōukān　　***N*: a weekly periodical; a weekly**

7. 零庫存 língkùcún

　　***N*: zero backlog; no additional inventory; no excess inventory**

8. 導致 dǎozhì　　***V*: to lead to; to result in; to cause**

常常看太小的字會導致眼睛近視。

Frequent reading of print which is too small can lead to near-sightedness.

9. 萎縮 wēisuō

　　***SV/N*: to atrophy; to dry up and shrink; to shrink back**

請問肌肉為什麼會萎縮？

May I ask why muscles can atrophy?

10. 多元化 dūoyuánhuà

　　***N*: pluralization; a plurality; divers; diversified**

現在的社會是多元化的，須要各種人才。

Modern society is a plurality (diversified); it requires every type of talent (talented individuals).

11. 相對 xiāngdùi

　　***A*: to undergo a relative change; to change in a related fashion**

大家的薪水增加了，相對的物價也升高了。

Everyone's salaries have increased;commodity prices, likewise, have also risen.

12. 打工 dǎgōng

VO: to do a part-time job or a job of short duration in order to earn some extra money; a summer job

大學生常常利用暑假去打工。

College students often take advantage of the summer vacation to go get a summer (part-time) job.

13. 外快 wàikuài　*N*: **extra income; spare income**

14. 忽視 hūshì　*V*: **to ignore; to neglect; to overlook**

人們常會忽視自己的健康。

People often neglect their own health.

15. 迎合 yínghé　*V*: **to cater to; to pander to**

他總是迎合老闆的意思。

He is always catering to the wishes of the boss.

16. 因應 yīnyìng　*V*: **to respond (to a change) to adjust**

社會變化太快，他不知道如何因應。

Society is changing too quickly; he does not know how to respond (to these changes).

17. 可觀 kěguān

AT: to be considerable; to be sizable; to be impressive

她的收入很可觀。

Her income is quite considerable.

18. 掏腰包 tāo yāobāo

VO: (literally: to pull out one's purse or pocket) to spend one's own money; to shell out cash; to make a contribution

逛街的時候很難不掏腰包。

When going for a stroll (i.e. window shopping) it is hard not to spend one's own money.

19. 言情小說 yánqíngxiǎoshuō *N*: a romance novel

20. 漫畫書 mànhuàshū *N*: comic books; graphic novels

21. 書卡 shūkǎ *N*: a book mark; a book marker

22. 加菲貓 jiāfēimāo

N: Garfield (a cartoon cat drawn by artist Jim Davis)

23. 專櫃 zhuānguì

N: a specialty counter in a store; a counter (department or section) of a department store responsible for the sale of a certain type of item (i.e. perfume, men's wear, etc.)

24. 柏青哥 buóqīnggē *N*: pachinko

25. 流連 liúlián

V: to be reluctant to leave; to be unwilling to part with

這裡的風景很好，使人流連忘返。

The scenery here is very nice; it makes people reluctant to leave (for home).

26. 品牌 pǐnpái

N: product trademark; name brand product (as in product consciousness)

27. 意˙識ˊ力ˋ yìshìli　*N*: consciousness; awareness

28. 產ˇ品ˇ chǎnpǐn　*N*: a product

29. 指ˇ名ˊ zhǐmíng

　　A: **to mention by name; to single out by name**

　　學校指名要我參加籃球比賽。

　　The school has singled me out by name to participate in the

　　basketball competition.

30. 闊ˋ綽ˋ kuòchuò

　　SV/AT: **to be living in luxury and extravagance; living in**

　　　　　　　luxury and extravagance

　　生活闊綽的人不一定很有錢。

　　People who live in luxury and extravagance are not neces-

　　sarily very rich.

31. 偶ˇ而ˊ（爾）ǒuér

　　A: **occasionally; sometimes; once in a long while**

　　我偶而吃一次牛排。

　　I occasionally eat a whole steak.

二、成語與俗語： Proverbs and Common Sayings:

1. 有ˇ錢ˊ有ˇ閒ˊ yǒuqián yǒuxián

　　to be idle and have a great deal of money; to have money and

　　time; to be part of the leisure class; the idle rich

　　社會上有錢有閒的人並不多。

　　There are not many people in society who are a part of the

leisure class.

2. 雨後春筍 yǔhòuchūnsǔn

(literally: to mushroom like bamboo shoots after rain) to expand dramatically; to grow rapidly

郊外的房子像雨後春筍般的蓋起來了。

Housing development in the suburbs has mushroomed like bamboo shoots after rain.

3. 生意興隆 shēngyì xīnglóng

business is brisk; business is booming

生意興隆是商人的理想。

To have brisk business is the dream of all business people.

4. 出手闊綽 chūshǒu kuòchuò

(literally: to leave one's hand like spilling water) to spend extravagantly; to throw money around; to waste money

他出手闊綽，引人注意。

His throwing money around caused people to take notice.

5. 討價還價 tǎojià huánjià

to bargain; to haggle over a price

在夜市買東西的人都免不了討價還價。

People who buy things at a night market cannot avoid haggling over prices.

三、句型：Sentence Patterns:

1. 隨著……，也相對……

along with X......, Y also reflects the change by......;

in the wake of X......, Y respectively has......;

in the same way as X......, Y has proportionally......

(1) 隨著科技的進步，玩具的品質也相對的提高。

(2) 隨著經濟的發展，休閒活動也相對的增加了。

(3) 隨著時光的流逝，孩子們也相對的長高了。

2. ⋯⋯以⋯⋯居多

of group X, Y is (are) in the majority.

(1) 住在海邊的人民，以捕魚為生的居多。

(2) 這個書店的書，以消遣性的作品居多。

(3) 青少年打工的地方，以速食店居多。

3. ⋯⋯不必太⋯⋯，反而⋯

......must not be too......, the result will then be......;

......should not be exceedingly......, this will then result in......;

......need not be (too)......, this will result in......

(1) 一部電影不必太長，大家反而喜歡看。

(2) 下雨不必太久，反而對農作物有益。

(3) 一個人不必太謙虛，反而使人容易接近。

4. 為了⋯⋯，不但⋯⋯，甚至⋯

......in order to......, not only......, (but) even go so far as to......;

......with the goal of......, not only......, (but) even......

(1) 他為了賺錢，不但晚上工作，甚至假日也工作。

(2) 為了迎合婦女的喜好，不但超級市場賣化妝品，甚至一般服
裝店也賣。

(3) 為了照顧生重病的孩子，她不但沒好好吃飯，甚至也沒上床
　　睡覺。

四、問題討論：Questions for Discussion:

1. 以成人為主的消費市場為何漸趨飽和？

　_____

2. 青少年為何有消費的潛力？

　_____

3. 哪些出版品受青少年歡迎？

　_____

4. 青少年喜歡流連的地方是哪些？

　_____

5. 為什麼對業者來說青少年是很好的顧客？

　_____

五、練習：Practice Exercises:

1. 選相似詞：（其中有複選）

Select the Word with the Same Meaning:

(1) 風潮：____　　*a.*潮水　*b.*潮流　*c.*風氣

(2) 導致：____　　*a.*造成　*b.*領導　*c.*疏導

(3) 忽視：____　　*a.*重視　*b.*輕視　*c.*忽略

(4) 財主：____　　*a.*富人　*b.*財產　*c.*房東

(5) 流連：____　　*a.*連續　*b.*徘徊　*c.*停留

(6) 闊綽：____　　*a.*闊氣　*b.*大方　*c.*寬大

2.造句：

Make Sentences:

(1) 潛力：_____

(2) 暢銷：_____

(3) 導致：_____

(4) 迎合：_____

(5) 因應：_____

(6) 流連：_____

(7) 雨後春筍：_____

(8) 討價還價：_____

(9) 外快：_____

(10) 隨著……也相對……：_____

3.寫相關字：

Write Related Words:

例：消費市場

超級市場

股票市場

外銷市場

(1) 少年週刊負責人

____ ____負責人

____ ____負責人

____ ____負責人

(2) 打工賺取外快

____賺取外快

　　　　＿＿＿賺取外快

　　　　＿＿＿賺取外快

　　(3) 言情小說

　　　　＿＿＿小說

　　　　＿＿＿小說

　　　　＿＿＿小說

　　(4) 服裝雜誌

　　　　＿＿＿雜誌

　　　　＿＿＿雜誌

　　　　＿＿＿雜誌

　　(5) 加菲貓是卡通人物

　　　　＿＿＿＿是卡通人物

　　　　＿＿＿＿是卡通人物

　　　　＿＿＿＿是卡通人物

4.分辨下列各字，加字成詞：

Differentiate the Characters Below and Combine them with Other Characters to Create Words or Phrases:

例：潮：新潮，潮水，風潮

　　朝：朝代，清朝，朝北

　　(1) 謹：＿＿＿＿＿＿＿＿＿＿＿＿＿

　　　　僅：＿＿＿＿＿＿＿＿＿＿＿＿＿

　　(2) 租：＿＿＿＿＿＿＿＿＿＿＿＿＿

　　　　祖：＿＿＿＿＿＿＿＿＿＿＿＿＿

　　(3) 傳：＿＿＿＿＿＿＿＿＿＿＿＿＿

　　　　轉：＿＿＿＿＿＿＿＿＿＿＿＿＿

(4) 型：_____

　　形：_____

(5) 嚮：_____

　　響：_____

(6) 購：_____

　　構：_____

(7) 淘：_____

　　陶：_____

(8) 貸：_____

　　貨：_____

(9) 濟：_____

　　齊：_____

(10) 壞：_____

　　環：_____

第十六課　新潮與保守

　　你是新潮①的，還是保守②的人？如果你有許多錢，會選擇怎樣的生活方式？有一些少年老成的人，雖然未必走在潮流③的尖端④，但他們謹守⑤傳統，是一群永不被淘汰⑥的人。

　　雅痞(Yuppies)⑦是近年來時髦的一群，他們努力工作，實現自我，同時拼命⑧賺錢，積極消費，其模式常常是住在租來的大房子或飯店中，不開伙，假日上健身院或到國外旅行。但社會上仍有另一種不同典型的人，他們喜歡家庭生活，重視親子關係，具有濃厚⑨的鄉土意識，表面上看來，雖不及雅痞新潮，然而他們卻是永不被時代淘汰的人。

　　這種尊重傳統的個性，使得他們做事相當的謹慎，必定先擬定⑩計畫。若有喜歡的物品，也會存錢購買。至於高價位，超過經濟範圍的東西，就會理性的打消念頭。對這種人來說，貸款如同負債，讓他們覺得好像芒刺在背。

　　其中有些人嚮往捏泥巴⑪、玩土的生活。多半會覺得在城市中購屋並不理想，如果可能的話，到鄉間蓋一棟別墅⑫，給自己和孩子一片菜圃⑬、花園。

　　其中有些人不喜歡隨遇而安、飄忽不定的生活方式，較具

我是新潮的人
努力工作、
積極消費、
不開伙、上健身院
國外旅行、
拼命賺錢、
住大飯店

我是保守的人
謹守傳統、
重視家庭及親子關係、
有濃厚鄉土意識、
視貸款如負債、
儲蓄置產、
維持現狀不輕易換工作

憂患意識，他們會不斷地努力增加存款數字，寧可將旅遊的錢省下，買些實用的家具。他們相信人有旦夕禍福，希望至少有兩名子女，並投保壽險⑭。這一切有時是因為缺乏安全感所造成的。這些人少年老成，會從年輕時就對人生做規畫，但過於實際。有時根本不願意給自己一點狂想⑮或野心⑯，只肯與性格相仿⑰的人來往，以保護自己的世界。

　　最令人擔憂的是很多機會到來時，可能暫時破壞了原有的安定生活，例如遇到調職⑱升遷⑲，這些人往往會忍痛割愛，以維持現狀，這是思想、做法極度保守的典型。

一、生詞：New Vocabulary:

1. 新ㄒㄧㄣ潮ㄔㄠˊ xīncháo　*SV/AT*: **to be trendy; to be avant-garde**

   他的思想很新潮。

   His thinking is very trendy.

2. 保ㄅㄠˇ守ㄕㄡˇ bǎoshǒu　*SV/AT*: **to be conservative**

   保守的人是不喜歡改革的。

   Conservative people do not like reforms.

3. 潮ㄔㄠˊ流ㄌㄧㄡˊ cháoliú　*N*: **a trend**

4. 尖ㄐㄧㄢ端ㄉㄨㄢ jiānduān

   AT/N: **the best of its kind; the peak; the cutting-edge; the acme**

   現在學習尖端科技的人越來越多了。

   At present more and more people are studying cuttingedge

technology.

5. 謹守 jǐnshǒu

> ***V***: **to faithfully adhere to; to staunchly uphold; to follow faithfully; to guard with care**
>
> 比賽時要謹守規則。
>
> During competitions rules should be faithfully adhered to.

6. 淘汰 táotài

> ***V/N/AT***: **to weed out; to eliminate the inferior (goods, contes-tants, etc.); to scour; to clear out**
>
> 在這競爭激烈的時代裡，不好的公司都會被淘汰。
>
> In this intensely competitive age, bad companies can all be weeded out.

7. 雅痞 yǎpǐ

> ***N***: **Yuppies (Young upwardly- mobile professionals)**

8. 拼命 pīnmìng

> ***VO***: **to risk one's life; to be reckless; to do (something) with all one's might; desperately; to overdo (something)**
>
> 拼命念書或工作的人常常忽略了健康。
>
> People who overdo their studies or their work often neglect their health.

9. 濃厚 nónghòu ***AT/SV***: **dense; thick; intense; strong**

> 他對下棋有濃厚的興趣。
>
> He has an intense interest in playing chess.

10. 擬定 (訂) nǐdìng

V: to draw up or map out (a plan)

在做一件大事以前，要先擬定一個計畫。

Before doing any large job, one should first draw up a plan.

11. 捏泥巴 niēníbā

VO: to make mud pies; to play in the mud; to play with mud (or clay)

小孩兒都喜歡捏泥巴。

Small children all like to make mud pies.

12. 別墅 biéshù　**N: a villa; a country house**

13. 菜圃 càipǔ　**N: a vegetable garden**

14. 壽險 shòuxiǎn　**N: life insurance**

15. 狂想 kuángxiǎng　**N/AT: frivolity; uninhibitedness**

16. 野心 yěxīn　**N: ambition**

17. 相仿 xiāngfǎng　**SV/AT: similar; about the same**

這兩個地方建築物的形式相仿。

The style of the buildings in these two places is similar

18. 調職 diàozhí　**VO: to transfer to a new post**

她調職了，所以她要搬家了。

She has been transferred to a new post; so she must move.

19. 升遷 shēngqiān

VO: to be promoted; to get transferred to a higher position

工作努力的人升遷得比較快。

People who work diligently are promoted more quickly.

二、成語與俗語： Proverbs and Common Sayings:

1. 少年老成 shàoniánlǎochéng

young but competent; accomplished though young; mature though young in years

少年老成的人比較穩重。

Young people who are competent are comparatively dignified.

2. 芒刺在背 mángcìzàibèi

(literally: to have sharp prickles in the back) to be worried; to be ill at ease

他欠了別人的錢，好像芒刺在背。

He owes other people money; it seems he is worried (because of it).

3. 隨遇而安 suíyùérān

to feel at ease under all circumstances

隨遇而安的人是最能適應新環境的。

The people who feel at ease under all circumstances are the (same) people most able to adapt to (new) environments.

4. 飄忽不定 piāohūbúdìng

(literally: to float about in the air without a fixed direction) to have no fixed address; to be transient

過了五年飄忽不定的生活，他已厭倦了，渴望安定下來。

Having spent five years of transient life, he is tired of it and longs to settle down.

5. 憂患意識 yōuhuàn yìshì

to be conscious of one's troubles or worries

生活經過困難的人比較有憂患意識。

People who have gone through difficulties in their lives are more concious of their troubles.

6. 旦夕禍福 dànxìhùofú

(literally: the good fortune and misfortune which may arise between dawn and dusk) unpredictable changes in one's fortune twists of fate

天有不測風雲，人有旦夕禍福。

Just as the Heavens have unpredictable weather; people have unpredictable changes in their fortunes.

7. 忍痛割愛 rěntònggēài

to reluctantly give up what one treasures; to bear with dignity the loss of what one cares for

他每賣出一張畫，就覺得是忍痛割愛。

Each painting that he sells makes him feel as though he is reluctantly giving up one of his treasures.

8. 維持現狀 wéichíxiànzhuàng

to maintain the status quo

如果目前的情況很好，那就維持現狀吧。

If the current situation is very good, then the status quo (should be) maintained.

三、句型：Sentence Patterns:

1. ……雖不及……，然而卻是…

X......although unable to meet the standards of......, nevertheless is......;

Though X does not come up to the expectations of......, it still in fact is......;

Although X is not up to the standards of......, nevertheless it is......

⑴ 這個博物館雖不及你們國家的，然而卻是我國最大的。

⑵ 他的中國工夫雖不及我，然而卻是孩子們喜歡的。

⑶ 他的智力雖不及其他的同學，然而卻是全班最用功的。

2. 若有……也會……

If X has Y......then X also would......;

If Y is available then X would......

⑴ 雖然她很節省，但若有合適的衣服，她也會買。

⑵ 你若有好的對象，也會結婚吧！

⑶ 我若有好的機會，也會出國留學。

3. 從……就……，但過於……

X from the time when......has always......, but......is excee-dingly......;

X ever since......always has......, however......has to excess......

⑴ 他從小就喜歡念書，但過於死記，不知活用。

⑵ 他從大學畢業後就不喜歡多說話了，但對人過於冷漠。

(3) 他從來就很多禮，但過於虛假。

四、易混淆的詞：Easily Confused Words:

1. 淘汰 táotài

   V/AT/N：to weed out; to eliminate the inferior (goods, contestants, etc.); to scour; to clear out

   沒有競爭心的人，會被淘汰。

   People without competitive spirit will be weeded out.

   排除 páichú

   V：to get rid of, to remove; to eliminate; to expel; to overcome (difficulty, fear, etc.)

   在動亂時代，人們不能排除憂患意識。

   In periods of upheaval, people cannot get rid of their awareness of misery.

   取消 qǔxiāo　　**V: to abolish; to cancel**

   下週的聚會取消了。

   The meeting next week has been canceled.

2. 尊重 zūnzhòng

   V/N: to venerate; to honor; to hold in reverence; to respect

   人人應該尊重別人的意見。

   Everybody should respect the views of other people.

   尊敬 zūnjìng

   V/N: to revere; to respect; respect; reverence

   受尊敬的人，一定有完美的人格。

People who are revered definitely have perfect moral character.

恭敬 gōngjìng *A/SV/N*: **to be respectful**

他對長輩很恭敬。

He is very respectful towards (his) seniors.

3. 規畫 guīhùa

V/N: **to map out or draw up (a plan); a plan; a scheme**

學校規畫了一套教學程序。

The school has drawn up a teaching program.

企畫 qihuà

V/N/AT: **to design; to lay out; to plan; to make a scheme**

貿易公司的企畫部常常得有新策略。

The trading company's planning department must often have new schemes.

計畫 jìhuà *V/N*: **to devise; to plan; a program; a plan**

暑假到了，家家都計畫一次遠程旅行。

Summer vacation has arrived; families have all planned long-distance trips.

4. 相仿 xiāngfǎng *SV/AT*: **to be similar**

掌中戲跟皮影戲的唱詞聽起來相仿。

"Zhang zhong xi" (a traditional Taiwanese form of puppet theater) and "pi ying xi" (a form of theater using shadow puppets) have lyrics which sound similar.

模仿 mófǎng *V*: **to imitate; to copy; to mimic**

他最會模仿別人說話。

He is very capable of mimicking (the way) other people speak.

仿冒 fǎngmào　*V/N*: **imitation; copied; fake**

仿冒品的價錢便宜很多。

The price for imitation products is much cheaper.

5. 維持 wéichí　*V*: **to preserve; to maintain; to keep**

你的中文能維持現狀就很好，不能退步啊！

If you can maintain your Chinese as it is, that would be excellent; do not fall behind!

保持 bǎochí　*V*: **to maintain; to keep**

開車的時候，應注意跟前後的車保持距離。

When driving a car one should pay attention to maintaining a distance from the cars in front and behind.

堅持 jiānchí　*V*: **to insist; to maintain unyieldingly**

他堅持要去冒這次險，勸他也不聽。

He insists he wants to go take this risk; he won't listen to any advice.

五、問題討論： Questions for Discussion:

1. 你是新潮的人？還是保守的人？

2. 雅痞是一群什麼樣的人？

3. 保守的人看見喜歡的物品但價錢太高會怎麼樣？

_____

4. 憂患意識是什麼？

_____

5. 保守的人有什麼優點？有什麼缺點？

_____

6. 雅痞有什麼優點？有什麼缺點？

_____

六、練習： Practice Exercises:

1. 選擇相似詞：（其中有複選）

Select the Word with the Same Meaning:

(1) 未必：_____　　a.不一定　b.不會　　c.不必

(2) 不開伙：____　　a.不吃飯　b.不做飯　c.不買飯

(3) 不及：_____　　a.不如　　b.來不及　c.比不上

(4) 謹慎：_____　　a.小心　　b.有耐心　c.粗心

(5) 貸款：_____　　a.代表　　b.存款　　c.借錢

(6) 性格：_____　　a.個性　　b.態度　　c.心情

(7) 令人：_____　　a.使人　　b.讓人　　c.命令

(8) 維持：_____　　a.保持　　b.支持　　c.堅持

(9) 極度：_____　　a.極端　　b.非常　　c.適度

2. 解釋：

Define the Following Terms:

(1) 潮流：_____

(2) 拼命：_____

(3) 淘汰：_____

(4) 貸款：_____

(5) 野心：_____

(6) 相仿：_____

(7) 維持現狀：_____

3. 填空：

Fill in the Blanks:

(1) 少年老成的人謹守____。

(2) 雅痞是近年來____的一群。

(3) 雅痞在假日時上____院或到國外____。

(4) 對保守的人來說貸款如同____，讓他們覺得____在背。

(5) 有些人希望到鄉間蓋一棟____，給自己和孩子一片____、花園。

(6) 有些人不喜歡____而安、____不定的生活方式。

(7) 具憂患____的人相信人有旦夕____，一定投保____險。

(8) 遇到調職升遷，保守的人往往會____割愛以維持現狀。

第十七課　人滿為患

　　地球在大宇宙①中只是一顆②光體③。這顆小小的光體上，竟有數不清的生物在生存④著，在不斷生長著。不說別的，現在只對人類來做一次探討，究竟這球體上的人類有多少呢？

　　根據報導，1987 年 7 月 11 日在南斯拉夫⑤誕生⑥了一個男嬰⑦，他是世界上第五十億⑧個人。再由資料上顯示，五十億人口剛好是 1950 年的兩倍；也就是說，在這三十七年中，世界人口有了這麼驚人的成長。那麼你能預估到 2020 年地球上有多少人口嗎？

　　為什麼世界上人口這麼快速地增加呢？其中原因大概可分兩方面來看，一是出生率⑨過高，二是死亡率⑩減低。於是人口的成長率就由幾何級數⑪不停地往上增加。在出生率過高的問題上，世界人口成長的趨勢有一十分明顯的現象，就是百分之十的人口，多半出生在開發中⑫國家與未開發⑬地區。人口的壓力使這些國家無法提高人民生活的品質與教育水準，因而引起了經濟問題、社會問題以及政治問題。例如非洲地方，人口的成長率高居世界之冠，尤其是在奈及利亞⑭最嚴重，有專家已預測說，到 2040 年奈國的人口將等於目前全非洲人口的總和⑮，

而且肯亞⑯在十七年內人口也將加倍成長。在這些地區中的國家，必須提高經濟成長率才能支持人口膨脹⑰的壓力。但是這點小希望，並不容易實現。因為這些多半依賴⑱農產品賺取⑲外匯⑳的國家，一旦受到國際市場的限制㉑，或者遭受天災人禍㉒，常常出現驚人的饑荒㉓。這樣怎能提高他們的經濟成長呢？在控制㉔出生率上，雖然也採用種種方法，如倡導節育㉕，或者限制出生（如一胎化㉖）。但都難有效實行，阻擋㉗不住人口膨脹的洪流㉘。

　　談到死亡率減低的原因也不少。因醫藥發達生活品質提高，注意環境衛生等等因素，使人口老化漸趨緩慢㉙，老年人口的比率日漸增多，形成了畸型㉚人口的壓力。在歐美及東南亞各國都逐漸成為死亡率減低的地區。在這種情形下，老年人成為依賴人口，加上兒童求學時期較長，奉養㉛老人及撫育㉜兒童的經濟活動人口反而不夠應付，形成了社會型態失衡㉝的現象。

　　近年來，我們看到日趨㉞嚴重的生態問題，大自然處處被破壞的問題。這人滿為患的地球，恐怕將不能成為宇宙中一顆閃亮㉟的光體了吧！

一、生詞：New Vocabulary：

1. 宇宙 yǔzhòu　*N*: the universe; the cosmos

2. 顆 kē　*M*: measure word for small roundish objects

　　天上有多少顆星，你能數得清嗎？

There are a number of stars in the sky; can you count them all?

3.　光體 guāngtǐ　*N*: celestial body (as in a planet)

4.　生存 shēngcún　*V*: to exist, to subsist

5.　南斯拉夫 Nánsīlāfū　*N*: Yugoslavia

6.　誕生 dànshēng

V: to come into being; to emerge; to be born

一千多年前的十二月有一個偉大的人誕生了。

In December over a thousand years ago a great individual was born.

7.　嬰 yīng　*N*: a baby; an infant

8.　億 yì　*M/N*: one hundred million; 100,000,000

你知道中國有幾億人口？

Do you know how many hundred millions of people constitute the population of China?

9.　出生率 chūshēnglǜ

N: the birth rate (the rate at which people are born)

10.　死亡率 sǐwánglǜ

N: the mortality rate; the death rate (the rate at which people die)

11.　幾何級數 jǐhéjíshù

N: geometric progression (an exponential increase)

12.　開發中 kāifāzhōng　*AT*: to be developing

開發中國家的經濟不斷地發展。

The economies of developing countries continuously grow.

13. 未開發 wèikāifā

AT: to be undeveloped; to be uncultivated

未開發國家人民的生活比較貧窮。

The life of people in undeveloped countries is comparatively poor.

14. 奈及利亞 Nàijílìyà　***PN*: Nigeria**

15. 總和 zǒnghé　***N*: the total; the sum; the sum total**

16. 肯亞 kěnyà　***PN*: Kenya**

17. 膨脹 péngzhàng

V/N: (*a*) to inflate; to expand; to swell

(*b*) inflation; expansion; swelling

喝水太多，肚子會膨脹。

Drinking too much water can expand the stomach.

18. 依賴 yīlài　***V*: to depend upon; to rely on**

二十多歲的人應該自立了，不可再存依賴心。

People over twenty years of age should stand on their own two feet; (they) cannot continue to be dependant (of a reliant mind).

19. 賺取 zhuànqǔ　***V*: to make (money); to earn (a salary)**

她每天替人照顧小孩，賺取自己的生活費。

Everyday she cares for the children of other people to earn her own living expenses.

20. 外匯 wàihùi　***N*: foreign exchange; foreign currency**

21. 限制 xiànzhì   *V/N*: to restrict, limit

22. 人禍 rénhuò

    N: human misfortune; man-made disaster; man-made calamity

23. 饑荒 jīhuāng   *N*: famine; crop-failure

24. 控制 kòngzhì   *V*: to control, to command

    現在許多人在控制飲食。

    Currently many people control eating.

25. 節育 jiéyù   *VO*: birth control

    中國大陸倡導節育，每對夫妻只可生一個孩子。

    Mainland China advocates birth control; each married couple can have only one child.

26. 一胎化 yìtāihuà

    N: (literally: single birth-ization) The practice of allowing only one child per family

27. 阻擋 zǔdǎng   *V/N*: to stop; to stem; to resist

    民主的潮流是無法阻擋的。

    There is no way to stem the tide of democracy.

28. 洪流 hóngliú   *N*: a mighty torrent; a powerful current

29. 緩慢 huǎnmàn   *AT/SV/A*: to be slow; slowly

    現在世界經濟的發展很緩慢。

    Currently the world's economic development is very slow.

30. 畸型 jīxíng

    AT: to be abnormal; to be deformed; to be malformed

懷孕時吃感冒藥，可能會生出畸型兒。

Taking cold medicine during pregnancy, one may give birth to a deformed child.

31. 奉養 fèngyàng　*V*: **to support (parents)**

兒女應該奉養年老的父母。

Children should support their parents in old age.

32. 撫育 fǔyù　*V*: **to rear; to bring up**

既然你生了孩子就要撫育他們。

Now that you have given birth to children you need to rear them.

33. 失衡 shīhéng　*V*: **to lose balance; to fall out of balance**

他走在獨木橋上，身體失衡，掉到河裡去了。

He was walking on a single-plank bridge, lost balance, and fell into the river.

34. 日趨 rìqū　*A*: **day by day**

35. 閃亮 shǎnliàng　*AT/V*: **to be shiny; to glitter; to glimmer**

她戴著一個閃亮的鑽戒。

She wore a glimmering diamond ring.

二、成語與俗語： Proverbs and Common Sayings:

1. 人滿為患 rénmǎnwéihuàn

a trouble of over population; to have a problem of overcrowding

世界上許多有名的大城市都人滿為患。

All over the world many of the famous large cities have a problem of overcrowding.

三、句型：Sentence Patterns:

1.……高居……之冠……

occupies the position of the........greatest; ....can be counted as the.......highest; ....is the highest in the.......; ....is the greatest in the.......

(1) 孟加拉的人口密度高居世界之冠。

(2) 這個城市的平均溫度高居全國之冠。

(3) 日本東京的物價高居世界之冠。

2.……等於……的總和

X is the equal of the sum total of Y;

X is equal to the sum of Y;

X is equivalent to the total of Y

(1) 中國的人口等於好幾個國家的總和。

(2) 他的收入等於我們全家收入的總和。

(3) 她家的院子很大，等於我和三家鄰居的總和。

3.……小小……竟……

such a small.......unexpectedly (is able to).......;

such a young.......actually (is able to).......

(1) 他小小年紀竟得到書法比賽的冠軍。

(2) 小小的一條船，竟能渡過這個海峽。

(3) 一隻小小的螞蟻竟能搬比牠身體重幾倍的東西。

4.……剛好是……(N) 倍

X is exactly (N) times the size of Y

(1) 這一國的人口剛好是哪一國的十倍。

(2) 他的收入剛好是我的兩倍。

(3) 這個學校剛好比那個學校大三倍。

5.……必須……，才能…

.......must......., the result will then be that.......; ....have to.......,
then can.......; ....need to......., then have a chance to.......

(1) 我們必須努力，才能成功。

(2) 你必須用功，才能考上好的大學。

(3) 你必須少吃，才能減肥。

四、易混淆的詞：Easily Confused Words：

1. 探討 tàntǎo

V/N: **to investigate; to study; to explore (possibilities, etc.);
to discuss (causes or effects, etc.)**

世界人口問題是值得探討的大問題。

The world population problem is a big problem worthy of
investigation.

檢討 jiǎntǎo

V/N: **to review and discuss (past performance, etc.); to search one's soul; to make a self-examination; to examine oneself**

批評別人前，先檢討檢討自己。

Before criticizing other people, (one should) first examine oneself.

2. 水準 shuǐzhǔn *N: a level; a standard*

各國政府盡力提升人民生活水準。

The government of every country does all it can to raise the standard of living of its people.

標準 biāozhǔn *N/AT: a criterion; a standard*

不合標準的產品不可銷到外國去。

Sub-standard (unable to meet the criterion for quality) products cannot be sold to foreign countries.

3. 阻擋 zǔdǎng *V: to resist; to stem; to block; to stop*

路上一輛汽車拋錨了，阻擋了後面不少車。

A car has broken down in the road, blocking quite a few cars behind it.

阻礙 zǔài *V: to hinder; to impede*

人口問題常阻礙了國家的經濟進步。

Population problems often hinder the economic progress of a country.

阻止 zǔzhǐ *V: to prevent; to hold back; to stop*

子女做了決定要做什麼，父母千萬別阻止。

(When) children have made a decision to do something, (their) parents should under no circumstances hold them back.

4. 依賴 yīlài

V/AT: to depend upon; to rely on; to be interdependent

太被寵愛的孩子多有依賴性。

Most children who have been doted on too much have (overly) dependent characters.

依-靠 yīkào　　*V*: **to rely on; backing; to support**

大學畢業了，不必再依靠父母了。

After graduation from university one should not rely on one's parents anymore.

五、問題討論：Questions for Discussion:

1. 為什麼世界人口增加的這麼快速？

---

2. 世界人口成長的趨勢有一個十分明顯的現象是什麼？

---

3. 為什麼說在開發中國家和未開發地區，想要提高經濟成長率來支持人口膨脹的壓力是很難的？

---

4. 人口壓力大，帶來什麼問題？

---

5. 死亡率減低的原因是什麼？

---

6. 歐美及東南亞各國死亡率減低有什麼問題？

六、練習：Practice Exercises:

1. 選相反詞：

Select the Word with an Opposite Meaning:

(1) 膨脹：＿＿＿　　*a.*萎縮　*b.*擴大　*c.*瘦小

(2) 饑荒：＿＿＿　　*a.*飢餓　*b.*豐收　*c.*荒涼

(3) 奉養：＿＿＿　　*a.*養活　*b.*遺棄　*c.*奉命

(4) 失衡：＿＿＿　　*a.*平衡　*b.*平均　*c.*衡量

(5) 閃亮：＿＿＿　　*a.*耀眼　*b.*閃閃　*c.*暗淡

2. 選相似詞 (其中有複選)：

Select the Word with a Similar Meaning:

(1) 究竟：＿＿＿　　*a.*到底　*b.*竟然　*c.*研究

(2) 預估：＿＿＿　　*a.*預測　*b.*預計　*c.*預言

(3) 水準：＿＿＿　　*a.*標準　*b.*水平　*c.*準備

(4) 阻擋：＿＿＿　　*a.*阻止　*b.*攔阻　*c.*擋住

(5) 限制：＿＿＿　　*a.*約束　*b.*範圍　*c.*控制

3. 造句：

Make Sentences:

(1) 幾何級數：＿＿＿＿＿＿＿＿＿＿＿＿＿＿＿＿＿

(2) 膨脹：＿＿＿＿＿＿＿＿＿＿＿＿＿＿＿＿＿＿＿

(3) 畸型：＿＿＿＿＿＿＿＿＿＿＿＿＿＿＿＿＿＿＿

(4) 撫育：＿＿＿＿＿＿＿＿＿＿＿＿＿＿＿＿＿＿＿

(5) 高居……之冠：＿＿＿＿＿＿＿＿＿＿＿＿＿＿＿

(6) 剛好是…… (N) 倍：＿＿＿＿＿＿＿＿＿＿＿＿＿

4.填空：

Fill in the Blanks:

⑴ 地球在_____中只是一顆光體。

⑵ 一九八七年七月十一日在_____誕生了世界上第_____個人。

⑶ 世界人口快速增加的原因，一是_____過高，二是_____減低。

⑷ 人口的成長率由_____不停地增加。

⑸ 人口的壓力使未開發地區無法提高人民生活的_____與教育_____。

⑹ 非洲地方人口的成長率_____世界之_____。

⑺ 有些地區常遭受____災____禍，常常出現驚人的_____。

⑻ 控制出生率的方法，有倡_____育，或_____胎化。

⑼ 醫藥發達，使人口老化漸趨_____。

⑽ 奉養_____及_____兒童形成了社會型態_____現象。

第十八課　十二生肖①

　　中國人除了姓名、籍貫②、性別之外，最重要的代表性標記就是「生肖」。也就是人人常互問的「你屬③什麼？」不論是年長的老公公老婆婆，或是剛上幼稚園的小朋友，他們都能清清楚楚地說出他屬哪一個生肖。生肖在中國人生活中確實④佔有一席之地，而且也是個人人津津樂道的話題。

　　在中國最早的文獻⑤中即載有不少有關十二生肖的傳說。中國傳統以十二地支⑥──子⑦、丑⑧、寅⑨、卯⑩、辰⑪、巳⑫、午⑬、未⑭、申⑮、酉⑯、戌⑰、亥⑱來代表年的代號，再選十二種動物去配合，不僅使人容易記住，也增加不少趣味性。

　　關於十二生肖的順序⑲怎麼排列成的呢？更有不少令人捧腹的故事。為什麼十二生肖沒有貓？為什麼十二生肖中老鼠排在第一位？現在介紹一個民間比較熟知的傳說，信不信由你。

　　從前有位玉皇大帝⑳要選十二種動物來配合十二地支，於是舉行賽跑，先到的十二名就按先後順序排下來。賽程中有一條河，不諳㉑水性的貓和鼠，就央求㉒老牛背他們過河。快到河邊時，為了爭第一，老鼠就把貓推下河心。接近岸邊時，老鼠

一躍㉓登上陸地，趕在牛的前面，得到第一。牛跟著上來，排在第二，隨後而來的是虎、兔、龍、蛇、馬、羊、猴、雞、狗、豬。貓不幸㉔落選㉕了，這個說法也告訴我們，為什麼貓跟鼠之間有那麼多的仇恨了。

在十二個生肖中，動物的形象也常印證㉖在人的個性舉止㉗上，比方說屬鼠的善於㉘節約儲蓄，較機警㉙；屬牛的外表悠閒㉚，內心固執㉛，屬虎的威風凜凜，十分勇敢；屬兔的性情溫和，容易跟人相處……。我們也時常聽人說：「我屬豬，我從來不吃豬肉。」「怪不得他那麼好吃懶做，原來他屬豬啊！」你仔細想想你的個性跟你的生肖有相像的地方嗎？

生肖文化並不只是中國人獨有的文化，因為生肖是一種圖騰獸㉜，也是一種年神㉝，像古埃及㉞、巴比倫㉟、非洲等地，也都有十二肖獸，只是各地所用的種類不同。古埃及的十二肖獸以貓為第一位呢！近年來在西方盛行的巴比倫星座㊱也傳到世界各地，年輕人之間，多以自己的星座來推測㊲運氣及當作擇友的參考。你是什麼星座，你自己知道吧！白羊㊳？金牛㊴？雙子㊵？天蟹㊶？天獅㊷？處女㊸？天秤㊹？天蠍㊺？射手㊻？山羊㊼？水瓶㊽？雙魚㊾？

中國人每逢新年總是喜歡迎接新的值年生肖，再加上各種吉利的讚詞㊿，如羊年代表吉祥(51)，馬年代表奔騰(52)，豬年象徵財富，……總之，年年都是如意吉祥的歲月。

一、生詞： New Vocabulary:

1. 生ㄕㄥ肖ㄒㄧㄠ shēngxiào

   N: One or all of the 12 symbols or signs of the Chinese horoscope. Each of these signs is represented by an animal. Unlike the Western horoscopic system which assigns a sign for a period of a month, the Chinese system assigns a sign for each year of a twelve-year cycle.

2. 籍ㄐㄧ貫ㄍㄨㄢ jíguàn   *N*: one's hometown; one's native soil

3. 屬ㄕㄨ shǔ

   V: to belong to (the sign of, etc.); to be governed by (the sign of, etc.)

   今年生的小孩屬雞。

   Children born this year are governed by the sign of the Rooster.

4. 確ㄑㄩㄝ實ㄕ quèshí   *A*: to be reliable; to be certain; to be true

   我確實不知道這件事是誰做的。

   I am certain that I do not know who did this thing.

5. 文ㄨㄣ獻ㄒㄧㄢ wénxiàn   *N*: document; literature

6. 地ㄉㄧ支ㄓ dìzhī

   N: The Terrestrial Branches used in calculation with the Celestial Stems; the 12 Chinese horoscopic symbols

7. 子ㄗ zǐ

   N: The first of the twelve Celestial Stems (horoscopic

signs). It is symbolized by the mouse.

8. 丑 chǒu

N: The second of the twelve Celestial Stems (horoscopic signs). It is symbolized by the ox.

9. 寅 yín

N: The third of the twelve Celestial Stems (horoscopic signs). It is symbolized by the tiger.

10. 卯 mǎo

N: The fourth of the twelve Celestial Stems (horoscopic signs). It is symbolized by the rabbit.

11. 辰 chén

N: The fifth of the twelve Celestial Stems (horoscopic signs). It is symbolized by the dragon.

12. 巳 sì

N: The sixth of the twelve Celestial Stems (horoscopic signs). It is symbolized by the snake.

13. 午 wǔ

N: The seventh of the twelve Celestial Stems (horoscopic signs). It is symbolized by the horse.

14. 未 wèi

N: The eighth of the twelve Celestial Stems (horoscopic signs). It is symbolized by the sheep.

15. 申 shēn

N: The ninth of the twelve Celestial Stems (horoscopic

signs). **It is symbolized by the monkey.**

16. 酉ⱼ yǒu

    N: **The tenth of the twelve Celestial Stems (horoscopic signs). It is symbolized by the chicken (or rooster).**

17. 戌ⱼ xū

    N: **The eleventh of the twelve Celestial Stems (horoscopic signs). It is symbolized by the dog.**

18. 亥ⱼ hài

    N: **The twelfth of the twelve Celestial Stems (horoscopic signs). It is symbolized by the pig.**

19. 順ⱼ序ⱼ shùnxù　　*N*: **an order; a sequence**

20. 玉ⱼ皇ⱼ大ⱼ帝ⱼ yùhuángdàdì

    PN: **The Jade Emperor, the supreme deity of Taoism**

21. 諳ⱼ ān

    V: **to be skilled in; to know well; to be versed in; to be fami-liar with**

    他因不諳法律，常常違法。

    Because he is not familiar with the law, (he) often breaks the law.

22. 央ⱼ求ⱼ yāngqiú　　*V*: **to beg; to implore; to entreat**

    他一遇到困難就央求朋友幫助。

    Whenever he encounters a difficulty, (he) begs his friends for help.

23. 躍ⱼ yuè / yaò　　*V*: **to jump; to leap; to spring; to bound**

這個人真厲害，一躍就過了牆。

This person is really fierce; (he) jumped over the wall in a single bound.

24. 不幸 búxìng *A*: **unfortunate; sad; unfortunately**

他不幸遇到車禍而斷了一條腿。

He unfortunately broke a leg in an automobile accident.

25. 落選 luòxuǎn

VO: **to lose an election; to not be selected; to be unable to make the list in an election**

這次選舉，王家三個兄弟都落選了。

In this election, the three brothers from the Wang family all lost.

26. 印證 yìnzhèng *V*: **to verify; to confirm; to corroborate**

我對他說的話有點懷疑，我要去印證一下。

I am a little doubtful about what he said; I want to (go) confirm it.

27. 舉止 jǔzhǐ *N*: **bearing; manner; behavior; air**

28. 善於 shànyú *V*: **to be adept at; to be good at**

貓善於捕捉老鼠。

Cats are good at catching mice.

29. 機警 jījǐng

SV/AT: **to be alert; to be quick-witted; to be sharp; to be vigilant**

山上的動物都很機警。

Mountain animals are all very alert.

30. 悠ㄡ閒ㄒㄧㄢ yōuxián

SV/AT: **to be leisurely; to be unhurried; to be carefree**

老年人應該過悠閒的生活。

Elderly people should pass leisurely lives.

31. 固ㄍㄨ執ㄓ gùzhí

SV/AT: **to be obstinate; to be stubborn; to be opinionated**

固執的人常常跟別人吵架。

Obstinate people often have quarrels with others.

32. 圖ㄊㄨ騰ㄊㄥ獸ㄕㄡ túténgshòu

N: **totemic animals; animals with religious or symbolic significance**

33. 年ㄋㄧㄢ神ㄕㄣ niánshén   *N*: **deities or spirits assigned to a year**

34. 埃ㄞ及ㄐㄧ Āijí   *PN*: **Egypt**

35. 巴ㄅㄚ比ㄅㄧ倫ㄌㄨㄣ Bābǐlún   *PN*: **Babylonia; Babylon**

36. 星ㄒㄧㄥ座ㄗㄨㄛ xīngzuò   *N*: **a constellation (of stars)**

37. 推ㄊㄨㄟ測ㄘㄜ tuīcè

V/N: **(*a*) to predict; to infer; to deduce; to guess; to conjecture**

(*b*) a prediction; an inference; a deduction; a guess; a conjecture

許多人推測明年的失業率會降低。

Many people predict that next year's unemployment rate will drop.

38. 白ㄅㄞˊ羊ㄧㄤˊ báiyáng

   N: **Aries (the ram) , a western astrological symbol (March 21-April 20)**

39. 金ㄐㄧㄣ牛ㄋㄧㄡˊ jīnniú

   N: **Taurus (the bull) , a western astrological symbol (April 21-May 21)**

40. 雙ㄕㄨㄤ子ㄗˇ shūangzi

   N: **Gemini (the twins), a western astrological symbol (May 22-June 21)**

41. 天ㄊㄧㄢ蟹ㄒㄧㄝˋ (巨ㄐㄩˋ蟹ㄒㄧㄝˋ) tiānxiè (jùxiè)

   N: **Cancer (the crab), a western astrological symbol (June 22-July 22)**

42. 天ㄊㄧㄢ獅ㄕ (獅ㄕ子ㄗˇ) tiānshī (shīzi)

   N: **Leo (the lion), a western astrological symbol (July 23-August 23)**

43. 處ㄔㄨˋ女ㄋㄩˇ chùnǔ

   N: **Virgo (the virgin), a western astrological symbol (August 24- September 23)**

44. 天ㄊㄧㄢ秤ㄔㄥˋ tiānchèng

   N: **Libra   (the balance),   a western astrological symbol (September 24- October 23)**

45. 天ㄊㄧㄢ蠍ㄒㄧㄝ tiānxiē

   N: **Scorpio (the scorpion), a western astrological symbol (October 24-November 22)**

46. 射手 (人馬) shèshǒu (rénmǎ)

    N: Sagittarius (the archer), a western astrological symbol (November 23- December 21)

47. 山羊 (魔羯) shānyáng (mójié)

    N: Capricorn (the goat), a western astrological symbol (December 22- January 20)

48. 水瓶 (水人) shuǐpíng (shuǐrén)

    N: Aquarius (the water bearer), a western astrological symbol (January 21-February 19)

49. 雙魚 shuāngyú

    N: Pisces (the fish), a western astrological symbol (February 20-March 20)

50. 讚詞 zàncí   *N*: **words of praise**

51. 吉祥 jíxiáng

    SV/AT: **to be auspicious; to be favorable; to be propitious; to be lucky**

    過年的時候一定要說吉祥話。

    During New Year's time one must definitely say auspicious things.

52. 奔騰 bēnténg

    FV: **to gallop (of a horse); to surge forward; to roll on in waves**

    她畫了一張萬馬奔騰的畫，很生動。

    She painted a picture of ten thousand horses galloping;

it was very vivid.

二、成語與俗語：Proverbs and Common Sayings:

1. 一席之地 yìxízhīdì

a place or position (which one occupies)

每個國家在國際舞臺上都佔有一席之地。

Every country occupies a place in the international arena.

2. 津津樂道 jīnjīnlèdào

to talk about with great relish; to take great delight in talking about

本校得了足球比賽第一名，全校師生都津津樂道。

This school won first place in the football match; all the teachers and students spoke about it with great relish.

3. 令人捧腹 lìngrénpěngfù

to make people hold their sides with laughter; to make others burst out laughing

爸爸說的笑話令人捧腹。

The joke father told made people hold their sides with laughter.

4. 威風凜凜 wēifēnglǐnlǐn

to be imposing; to be awe-inspiring

大將軍騎在一匹高大的白馬上真是威風凜凜。

A great general riding on a great, white horse is really awe-inspiring.

三、句型 : Sentence Patterns:

1. 除了……最重要的是……

besides......the most important thing is......;

aside from......the most crucial thing is......

(1) 你除了好好念書以外,最重要的是注意身體的健康。

(2) 過馬路時除了看看兩邊的車子,最重要的是遵守交通規則。

(3) 媽媽除了照顧小孩的衣食以外,最重要的是注意他們的教育。

2. ……確實……而且也是

it is true that......, moreover, it is also true that......;

......certainly is......, in addition, it is also certain that......

(1) 她確實漂亮,而且也是個能幹的人。

(2) 這裡的山水確實很美,而且也是空氣最好的地方。

(3) 這個大學的設備確實很好,而且也是人才最多的學校。

3. 並不只是……也是……

......X really is not only for......, X is also for......;

......X does not just......, X is also for......;

......X is not only......, X is also......

(1) 工作並不只是賺錢,也是一種樂趣。

(2) 球類比賽並不只是鍛鍊身體,也是訓練大家的團隊精神。

(3) 學校並不只是傳授知識的地方,也是培養良好品德的處所。

四、易混淆的詞：Easily Confused Words:

1. 話題 huàtí

N: the theme of a conversation; a topic of conversation

男生多以女生的事為話題。

Boys often take girls as a topic of conversation.

題目 tímù　**N: a topic; a subject; a title**

他講演的題目很專業化。

The topic of his lecture was very specialized.

談話 tánhuà

VO: a statement; a chat; a talk; a conversation

今天開會人數不夠，只算是談話會。

There were not enough people at the meeting today; it can only be considered a chatting session.

2. 趣味 qùwèi

N/AT: an interest; a delight; a taste for; a liking for

有趣味的事，多半是引人喜愛或叫人發笑的。

Most delightful things make people enjoy them or cause them to laugh.

興趣 xìngqù

N: an enthusiasm for; an eagerness to; an interest

他的興趣很廣泛。

His interests are very wide-ranging.

3. 順序 shùnxù

N: **to take turns; a sequence; ordered; to do something in proper order**

按著大小、長幼排列叫順序。

Things organized on the basis of size (largest to smallest) or age (oldest to youngest) are called ordered (i.e. are in sequence).

次ㄘ序ㄒㄩ cìxù　*N*: **a succession; an order; a sequence**

排隊買票，要按先後次序。

When lining up to buy tickets (tickets will be sold) from the first to last in succession.

秩ㄓ序ㄒㄩ chìxù　*N*: **arrangement; order**

上課的秩序好，老師比較講得愉快。

When the classes are orderly, teachers can lecture more happily.

4. 推ㄊㄨㄟ測ㄘㄜ tūicè　*V/N*: **to infer; to conjecture; to guess**

由 1992 年的出生率可以推測到十年後的人口總數。

From the 1992 birth rate (figures) one can guess at on the total population ten years from then.

預ㄩ測ㄘㄜ yùcè　*V/N*: **to forecast; to calculate**

地震不可以預測什麼時候發生。

When an earthquake will occur cannot be forecast.

5. 值ㄓ年ㄋㄧㄢ zhínián

AT: **to be something for a year; to act as something on a yearly basis**

中國以十二種動物當作每年的值年代表。

China uses twelve animals to represent the years.

值ㄓ班ㄅㄢ zhíbān　**VO: to be on duty; to be on the shift**

他今晚不回家，在公司值班。

He won't return home this evening; (he) is on duty at the company.

輪ㄌㄨㄣ值ㄓ lúnzhí　***A/V*: to take turns; to go on duty in turns**

我家七個人每週輪值一次洗碗。

The seven people in my family take turns washing the bowls (dishes) once each week

五、問題討論：Questions for Discussion:

1. 十二生肖是怎麼來的？順序是怎麼排列的？

_____

2. 你認為你的個性跟你的生肖確實有相像的地方嗎？

_____

3. 年輕人喜歡用星座來做什麼？你相不相信？為什麼？

_____

4. 中國人喜歡迎接新的值年生肖，代表什麼意義？

_____

5. 你認為虎、兔、龍、猴、雞、狗各代表什麼？

_____

六、練習：Practice Exercises:

1. 配合題：

Matching:

(1) 子、丑 (　　) 　　　　　a. 虎、兔

(2) 寅、卯 (　　) 　　　　　b. 馬、羊

(3) 辰、巳 (　　) 　　　　　c. 狗、豬

(4) 午、未 (　　) 　　　　　d. 鼠、牛

(5) 申、酉 (　　) 　　　　　e. 龍、蛇

(6) 戌、亥 (　　) 　　　　　f. 貓、魚

(7) 羊　　 (　　) 　　　　　g. 猴、雞

(8) 豬　　 (　　) 　　　　　h. 鹿、狐

　　　　　　　　　　　　　i. 吉祥

　　　　　　　　　　　　　j. 財富

　　　　　　　　　　　　　k. 奔騰

2.造句：

Make Sentences:

(1) 節約：＿＿＿＿＿＿＿＿＿＿＿＿＿＿＿＿

(2) 機警：＿＿＿＿＿＿＿＿＿＿＿＿＿＿＿＿

(3) 印證：＿＿＿＿＿＿＿＿＿＿＿＿＿＿＿＿

(4) 舉止：＿＿＿＿＿＿＿＿＿＿＿＿＿＿＿＿

(5) 津津樂道：＿＿＿＿＿＿＿＿＿＿＿＿＿＿

3.選擇：

Choose the Appropriate Phrase:

清清楚楚　　　一席之地　　　津津樂道

令人捧腹　　　先後次序　　　不幸落選

節約儲蓄　　　內心暴躁　　　性情溫和

(1) 屬牛的人常是外表悠閒＿＿＿＿＿。

⑵ 他講的笑話真是 _____ ，人人都在哈哈大笑。

⑶ 母親都能 _____ 說出自己孩子的生肖，不會錯。

⑷ 中國傳統十二地支的說法在曆書上佔有 _____ 。

⑸ 孩子躍登第一名，總是父母 _____ 的得意事。

⑹ 故事中貓被推下河心，所以貓在中國十二生肖中 ___ 。

⑺ 善於理財的人多喜歡 _____ 。

⑻ 他家兄弟四人按 _____ 都已結婚了。

⑼ _____ 的人不容易跟別人吵架。

第十九課　救濟①與自立②

　　無論資本主義③、社會主義④或第三世界的國家，也無論漁牧⑤狩獵⑥社會或科技⑦發達的現代文明生活，都有「貧窮」的存在，只是以不同的型式顯現出來而已。

　　對於貧民的救助政策應採取選擇式的或是普遍性的尚無定論。雖然大部分學者認為普遍性較優，但在面對有限的資源壓力下，不得不界定⑧貧窮的測量⑨方法，即一般所謂的貧窮線，低於該標準者才能申請⑩各項補助⑪。

　　有些國家和地區經歷了所謂的福利權利運動。這個運動，不僅提高了申請社會救助者被核准⑫救助的機會，更造成被救助者在心態上和行為上的改變。申請救助者在排隊申請時不再是謙卑⑬的或低聲下氣的，而是用非常氣憤⑭和苛責⑮的口吻⑯、憤怒的心情、不耐煩的態度來對待為他們服務的人員。

　　福利國家曾是多少人盼望而爭取的，人民所信仰的利他性，互助互惠精神，曾是一種被宣揚⑰的美德，但在這種沒有相對責任的福利權利風行後，又怎能期待受救助者自助自救而脫離⑱貧窮？

　　福利權利的擴張帶來的後遺症⑲，破壞了原先福利國家的

理念⑳和消滅貧窮的憧憬㉑，而且這種自動可得的社會福利，也造成家庭解體㉒的主要因素，父親毫無愧疚㉓或罪惡感地遺棄㉔妻子和小孩，因為他們知道福利國家會妥善㉕照顧這些被棄的婦孺㉖。人類原本高貴的情操㉗，自給自足的尊嚴㉘，犧牲㉙、努力的堅忍㉚意志被破壞無遺，對於福利的依賴越來越深，而且有恃無恐。

　　總之，解決貧窮問題採取最簡單最直接的經濟救助路線，不是一條正確的途徑㉛。因為這樣不僅造成更多的福利依賴者，更嚴重的是導致價值觀的危機與家庭倫理的破壞。現在有的國家採取「以工代賑」(給貧戶簡單的工作，以賺取基本工資) 或給貧戶辦理職業訓練，試圖㉜增進其工作能力，恢復其自信心及責任感，但其中也充滿了爭辯㉝和困難。如何依文化背景、社會結構、經濟成長等規畫出一個適中的解決或舒緩㉞貧窮的有效策略，是大家應該審慎㉟思考的課題。

一、生詞：New Vocabulary：

1. 救濟 jiùjì　　*VO/N*: to provide relief; to relieve; to succor

   世界各地有許多難民須要救濟。

   Every part of the world has many refugees who require relief.

2. 自立 zìlì

   SV/AT: able to stand on one's own; self-supporting; independent; self-sustaining

他先接受救濟，經過一段時間就自立了。

First he received relief, then after a while he was able to stand on his own.

3. 資本主義 zīběnzhǔyì *N*: capitalism

4. 社會主義 shèhuìzhǔyì *N*: socialism

5. 漁牧 yúmù

   AT/N: to use fishing and animal herding (to raise what one eats); fishing and animal husbandry

6. 狩獵 shòuliè

   AT/N: to use hunting to gather what one eats; hunting

7. 科技 kējì *AT/N*: science and technology; technology

   現在是科技發達的時代。

   Now is a period of technological development.

8. 界定 jièdìng

   V: to classify; to delimit; to set terms by which to define something

   各國界定貧窮的方法不完全相同。

   Each country's methods for classifying the poor are not exactly the same.

9. 測量 cèliáng *V*: to measure; to survey

   他正在測量這座山的高度。

   He is in the midst of measuring the height of this mountain.

10. 申請 shēnqǐng *V/N*: to apply for

    你知道申請獎學金的條件嗎？

Do you know the requirements to apply for a scholarship?

11. 補助 bǔzhù

V/N: (a) to subsidize; to give an allowance; to provide monetary assistance

(b) a subsidy; an allowance; monetary assistance

遭受火災、風災、水災的家庭，可申請補助。

Families which have suffered from a fire, a hurricane (a wind related disaster) or a flood (a water related disaster) can apply for monetary assistance.

12. 核准 hézhǔn

V/N: (a) to approve

(b) approval

他申請補助已被核准了。

He applied for monetary assistance and has already received approval (for it).

13. 謙卑 qiānbēi

SV/AT: to be humble; to be self-depreciating

他的態度總是那麼謙卑。

His attitude is always so humble.

14. 氣憤 qìfèn　**SV/AT: to be furious; to be indignant**

任何人遭受不公平待遇時，都會氣憤。

Any person who receives unfair treatment is sure to be indignant.

15. 苛責 kēzé

V/AT: **to be harsh and demanding; to be severely critical**

孩子考試的成績不大好，但他已經很用功，我不忍心苛責
他。

The child's test grades are not particularly good, but he is
already very hard-working; I do not have the heart to be
severely critical of him.

16. 口吻 kǒuwěn

N: **tone; connotation of what is being said**

17. 宣揚 xuānyáng

V: **to advocate; to propagate; to promote**

牧師在宣揚教義

The pastor is advocating the doctrines of his religion.

18. 脫離 tuōlí

V: **to break away from; to divorce oneself from; to separate oneself from**

他認為信教可以脫離煩惱。

He believes that by believing in religion one can break away
from one's worries.

19. 後遺症 hòuyízhèng

N: **The aftermath of a disease or accident; the after-effects of a disease or an accident; a side-effect; an after-effect**

20. 理念 lǐniàn　　*N*: **a rational concept; rationality**

21. 憧憬 chōngjǐng

V/N: (**a**) **to long for; to yearn for something or someplace**

(**b**) **a yearning; a longing for something or someplace**

她憧憬著美麗的未來。

She longs for a beautiful future.

22. 解體 jiětǐ

V/N: (**a**) **to fall apart; to disintegrate**

(**b**) **disintegration**

這個組織解體了，因為大家太自私。

This organization is falling apart because everyone is too selfish.

23. 愧疚 kuìjiù

SV/AT: to suffer from a guilty conscience; to feel a sense of guilt; to feel pangs of shame

他做錯了事覺得很愧疚。

He did something wrong, so he feels a sense of guilt.

24. 遺棄 yíqì

V: to abandon; to for sake; to leave uncared-for

遺棄太太和兒女的男人實在太不負責。

The men who abandon their wives and children truly are selfish and irresponsible.

25. 妥善 tuǒshàn

AT/SV/A: to be proper; to be appropriate; to be fitting

多數父母會妥善照顧自己的子女。

Most parents will properly care for their children.

26. 婦ㄈㄨˋ孺ㄖㄨˊ fùrú　*N*: women and children

27. 情ㄑㄧㄥˊ操ㄘㄠ qíngcāo

　　N: moral integrity; sentiment; sensibilities

28. 尊ㄗㄨㄣ嚴ㄧㄢˊ zūnyán　*N*: dignity; honor

29. 犧ㄒㄧ牲ㄕㄥ xīshēng

　　V/N: (*a*) to sacrifice; to lay down (one's life) for something

　　　　(*b*) a sacrifice

許多軍人為保衛國土而犧牲了。

Many soldiers have laid down their lives to protect their national territory.

30. 堅ㄐㄧㄢ忍ㄖㄣˇ jiānrěn

　　SV/AT: to be determined; to be dedicated; to have fortitude; to be steadfast and persevering; determination; dedication; fortitude

他有堅忍的意志，不會動搖。

He has a determined will; he will not waver.

31. 途ㄊㄨˊ徑ㄐㄧㄥˋ tújing　*N*: a channel; a way; a path

32. 試ㄕˋ圖ㄊㄨˊ shìtú　*V/A*: to try; to attempt

敵人試圖攻佔我們的土地。

The enemy is trying to occupy our soil.

33. 爭ㄓㄥ辯ㄅㄧㄢˋ zhēngbiàn

　　V/N: (*a*) to dispute; to argue; to debate

　　　　(*b*) a dispute; an argument; a debate

常常為小事爭辯的人浪費了很多時間。

People who often argue over small matters waste a lot of time.

34. 舒緩 shūhuǎn　　*V*: **to relax; to take one's leisure**

喝一杯熱茶，可以舒緩緊張的情緒。

Drinking a cup of hot tea can relax (one when one is in) a tense mood.

35. 審慎 shěnshèn　　*SV/A*: **to be cautious; to be careful**

我們應該審慎研究這個問題。

We should carefully research this problem.

二、成語與俗語：Proverbs and Common Sayings:

1. 尚無定論 shàngwúdìnglùn

to still remain an open (un-answered) question; to be unresolved; to be without a final conclusion

患癌症的原因，尚無定論。

The cause of contracting cancer still remains an open question.

2. 互助互惠 hùzhùhùhuì

to be mutually beneficial; to help each other

我們要組織一個團體，以互助互惠為目的。

We want to organize an organization with mutual assistance as its objective.

3. 自給自足 zìjǐzìzú

to be self-sufficient; to be self-supporting

這個國家的糧食可以自給自足，但是石油必須買外國的。

(In regards to food) this country is self-sufficient, but (its) oil must be purchased abroad.

4. 破壞無遺 pòhuàiwúyí

to be damaged beyond repair; to be unrecoverably ruined

這些寺廟的神像被破壞無遺。

The images (paintings and statues) of the gods in these temples have been damaged beyond repair.

5. 有恃無恐 yǒushìwúkǒng

there is no fear when one has something to fall back upon; to be fearless because on has strong backing

明天的考試他有恃無恐，因為他很早就開始預備了。

He has no fears about tomorrow's test, because he started preparing (for the test) very early; he has something to fall back upon.

6. 以工代賑 yǐgōngdàizhè

(literally: to use work to act as relief) public works projects which give the poor and unemployed an opportunity to earn a living; to relieve people in disaster areas by giving them employment instead of an outright grant

有人認為「以工代賑」是最好的救濟窮人的方法。

Some people believe that "to use work to act as relief" is the best way to provide relief for the poor.

三、句型：Sentence Patterns:

1. 雖然……但……，不得不……

although......nevertheless......, ...have no choice but to......

(1) 雖然他很努力，但考不上大學，不得不去工作。

(2) 雖然他喜歡這個公司，但老闆對他不公平，他不得不離開。

(3) 她雖然想開一家書店，但本錢太少，不得不放棄。

2. 不僅……更……

......not only......in addition......;

......not just......moreover......

(1) 她不僅會跳舞，更會彈琴。

(2) 我的家鄉不僅有青山更有綠水。

(3) 這棵樹不僅開美麗的花，更結好吃的果。

3. ……不再……，而是……

......(contrary to what might be expected) is no longer ......but is in fact......;

......(unlike what one might expect) does not......but in reality does......

(1) 他不再是一個商人而是一個律師。

(2) 他不再騙人，而是一個誠實的人。

(3) 這個學校不再只收本地生，而是各種民族的學生都收。

四、易混淆的詞：Easily Confused Words:

1. 謙卑 qiānbēi

***SV/AT*: to be humble; to be self-depreciating**

他太謙卑小看自己了。

He is too humble and belittles himself.

謙虛 qiānxū

***SV/AT/N*: to be modest; to be unassuming; to be selfeffacing**

中國人過分謙虛是客氣的表示。

The excessive modesty of Chinese people is an expression of politeness.

2. 苛責 kēzé

***V*: to be harsh and demanding; to be severely critical**

對孩子不可太苛責，否則會離家出走。

One cannot be too harsh and demanding of children; otherwise, they may leave home.

責備 zébèi

***V/N*: to reprimand; to upbraid; to reproach; to blame**

員工做錯事，老闆責備幾句就算了。

(When) the staff does something wrong, the boss reprimands them with a few words (a few sentences) and then it is over with.

責罰 zéfá   ***V/N*: to punish; a punishment**

父母為愛而責罰子女。

The punishment is not only a reprimand; physical punishment or monetary punishment is also used as a (disciplinary) warning.

3. 宣揚 xuānyáng

V: to advocate; to propagate; to promote

佛教宣揚佛祖慈悲濟眾的教義。

Buddhism advocates the Buddhist patriarch's (sakyamuni's)
religious doctrine of benevolence and aiding the masses.

表揚 biǎoyáng

**V/AT: to cite for all to know; to publicly praise; to com-
mend**

學校表揚成績優秀的好學生。

The school publicly praises good students of outstanding
achievements.

張揚 zhāngyáng

**V: to make public something which should not be made
known (e.g. a scandal, a secret, etc.); to publicize un-
necessarily.**

有些不名譽的事，別張揚出去

Some dishonorable things should not be made public.

4. 遺棄 yíqì

V/AT: to abandon; to forsake; to leave uncared for

被父母遺棄的孩子，社會上有好心的人去撫養。

Society has good-hearted people who go and raise children
left uncared for by their fathers or mothers.

拋棄 pāoqì　**V: to desert; to discard; to forsake**

週末我們該拋棄繁忙的工作，到郊外休閒一番。

On weekends we should leave our troublesome work and go out to the suburbs to rest.

放⁵棄⁵ fàngqi *V*: **to renounce; to give up; to abandon**

這是你的選舉權利，你怎麼可以放棄呢！

This is your right to vote; how can you renounce it?

五、問題討論： Questions for Discussion:

1. 對於貧民的救助政策目前採取哪一種方式？

_____

2. 福利權利運動有什麼優點缺點？

_____

3. 解決貧窮問題採取經濟救助路線為什麼不是一條正確的路線？

_____

4. 「以工代賑」是什麼意思？有什麼好處？

_____

5. 你認為解決或舒緩貧窮的有效策略是什麼？

_____

六、練習： Practice Exercises:

1. 將生詞連成句子：

Combine the Following Words with New Vocabulary to Make Sentences:

(1) 採取

選擇式 } _____

普遍性

(2) 謙卑
　　苛責　　}　＿＿＿＿＿＿＿＿＿＿＿
　　口吻　　　＿＿＿＿＿＿＿＿＿＿＿

(3) 期待
　　自助自救　}　＿＿＿＿＿＿＿＿＿
　　貧窮　　　＿＿＿＿＿＿＿＿＿＿＿

(4) 愧疚
　　遺棄　　}　＿＿＿＿＿＿＿＿＿＿
　　罪惡感　　＿＿＿＿＿＿＿＿＿＿＿

(5) 導致
　　倫理　　}　＿＿＿＿＿＿＿＿＿＿
　　破壞　　　＿＿＿＿＿＿＿＿＿＿＿

2. 分辨下列各詞並造句：

Differentiate the Following Words and Use Them in Sentences:

(1) 發達：＿＿＿＿＿＿＿＿＿＿＿＿＿＿

　　發現：＿＿＿＿＿＿＿＿＿＿＿＿＿＿

　　發明：＿＿＿＿＿＿＿＿＿＿＿＿＿＿

　　發生：＿＿＿＿＿＿＿＿＿＿＿＿＿＿

(2) 普遍：＿＿＿＿＿＿＿＿＿＿＿＿＿＿

　　普通：＿＿＿＿＿＿＿＿＿＿＿＿＿＿

(3) 壓力：＿＿＿＿＿＿＿＿＿＿＿＿＿＿

　　壓迫：＿＿＿＿＿＿＿＿＿＿＿＿＿＿

(4) 權利：＿＿＿＿＿＿＿＿＿＿＿＿＿＿

　　權力：＿＿＿＿＿＿＿＿＿＿＿＿＿＿

(5) 補助：＿＿＿＿＿＿＿＿＿＿＿＿＿＿

補習：＿＿＿＿＿＿＿＿＿＿＿＿＿＿＿＿

(6) 尊嚴：＿＿＿＿＿＿＿＿＿＿＿＿＿＿＿＿

尊敬：＿＿＿＿＿＿＿＿＿＿＿＿＿＿＿＿

嚴重：＿＿＿＿＿＿＿＿＿＿＿＿＿＿＿＿

(7) 努力：＿＿＿＿＿＿＿＿＿＿＿＿＿＿＿＿

用功：＿＿＿＿＿＿＿＿＿＿＿＿＿＿＿＿

(8) 堅忍：＿＿＿＿＿＿＿＿＿＿＿＿＿＿＿＿

堅固：＿＿＿＿＿＿＿＿＿＿＿＿＿＿＿＿

(9) 爭辯：＿＿＿＿＿＿＿＿＿＿＿＿＿＿＿＿

辯論：＿＿＿＿＿＿＿＿＿＿＿＿＿＿＿＿

(10) 有效：＿＿＿＿＿＿＿＿＿＿＿＿＿＿＿＿

效果：＿＿＿＿＿＿＿＿＿＿＿＿＿＿＿＿

效率：＿＿＿＿＿＿＿＿＿＿＿＿＿＿＿＿

3.解釋：

Define the Following Terms:

(1) 資本主義：＿＿＿＿＿＿＿＿＿＿＿＿

(2) 社會主義：＿＿＿＿＿＿＿＿＿＿＿＿

(3) 以工代賑：＿＿＿＿＿＿＿＿＿＿＿＿

(4) 後遺症：＿＿＿＿＿＿＿＿＿＿＿＿＿

(5) 狩獵：＿＿＿＿＿＿＿＿＿＿＿＿＿＿

(6) 有恃無恐：＿＿＿＿＿＿＿＿＿＿＿＿

(7) 互助互惠：＿＿＿＿＿＿＿＿＿＿＿＿

(8) 自給自足：＿＿＿＿＿＿＿＿＿＿＿＿

第二十課　我寫「乾」你寫「干」

　　中國文字的演變①，可以說始自殷商②甲骨文③，繼之而起的是刻在銅器上的金文④。自秦始皇⑤統一中國文字以後，大篆⑥、小篆⑦逐漸出現了。到了漢朝⑧，工工整整的隸書⑨又十分盛行。尤其在筆、墨⑩、紙、硯⑪(俗稱文房四寶）發明以後，普遍使用，使中國文字有了更大的進步。凡是楷書⑫、行書⑬、草書⑭，都被中國人視為又實用又藝術的書寫文字。印刷體⑮的正楷⑯，方方正正一筆不苟。書法體的行書、草書，看起來龍飛鳳舞，如行雲流水一般，成為富有典雅⑰美感的書法藝術。從此中國文字有簡有繁，全憑個人習性和愛好，簡繁通用，極易辨認⑱。這種傳統的中國文字實在具有不可磨滅的藝術價值。

　　然而自中國大陸通行簡體字後，使數千年來中國文字有了很大的改變。當然在中國大陸為了眾多的十一億人口，文字的簡化是減少文盲較有效的辦法。此時期簡體字也確實發揮不少功能。但近四十年來大陸上的新生代，在暢遊名勝古蹟時，竟然看不太懂碑銘⑲匾額⑳上的題字㉑。再接觸到古籍經典㉒時，更是茫然不解。一旦臺灣海峽兩岸正式來往以後，簡字繁字問題也增加不少接觸時的困擾。如旅遊的解說、商務的契約、來往

的文件等等。

　　一般而言，簡體字的形成多半根據行書的結構而造出的。比方說：「言」旁㉓寫成「讠」，「會」寫成「会」，「應」寫成「应」，「體」寫成「体」……這一類的字，實行起來仍能被人接受，但有些字確實令人覺得有商榷㉔的必要。譬如：「干」可以代替「乾」、「幹」，只會寫簡體字的人把「乾淨」寫成「干淨」，或把「幹什麼」寫成「干什麼」。

　　除此以外，尚有一些很有神秘㉕性的簡體字。如「尘」、「灭」、「卫」、「厂」、「币」、「发」、「导」、「开」、「关」、「业」，用習慣了的人也不覺得奇怪，但是一旦讓一向使用繁體字的人看，真的想半天也猜不出呢！以目前的情形來看，海峽兩岸的中國人，只有我寫我的「乾」，你寫你的「干」了。

一、生詞：New Vocabulary:

1. 演變 yǎnbiàn　*V/N*: to develop and change; to evolve

   一個小問題，慢慢演變為大問題。

   One small problem slowly evolves into a large problem.

2. 殷商 yīnshāng

   N: The Shang Dynasty (circa. 1800 - 1200 BC.). Later re-named the Yin Dynasty.

3. 甲骨文 jiǎgǔwén

   N: Oracle Bones; ancient carvings in bone (most often tortoise shell or the collar bones of oxes) which contain the earliest known samples of recognizable Chinese characters. It is believed that these items were used for divination purposes; hence the name "Oracle Bones".

4. 金文 jīnwén   *N*: ancient inscriptions on bronze

5. 秦始皇 Qínshǐhuáng   *N*: (246-214 BC.)

The founder (and one of two rulers) of the Qin Dynasty (which rose after the Zhou Dynasty). He is considered responsible for (among other things) the building of the Great Wall and the first unification of the territories now considered to make up modern China. However, his dictatorial regime was so oppressive that his dreams of an eternal dynasty died with him (his son only ruled for three years after his death) and he is remembered to this day only by the mocking name "The First Emperor of Chin".

6. 大篆 dàzhuàn

N: the "great seal"characters-an ancient calligraphic style in use before the period of the Chin Dynasty

7. 小篆 xiǎozhuàn

N: the "small seal"characters-an ancient calligraphic style which replaced the "great seal"character style during the time of the Chin Dynasty.According to popular belief, this style was forced into use by "The First Emperor of Chin" during his reign in order to standardize the Chinese writing style.

8. 漢朝 hàncháo　*N*: the Han Dynasty (206 BC. - 219 AD.)

9. 隸書 lìshū

N: The clerical style of Chinese calligraphy popular during the Han Dynasty

10. 墨 mò　*N*: ink; ink stick

11. 硯 yàn

N: inkstone; inkslab (used for mixing and holding ink for Chinese calligraphy)

12. 楷書 kǎishū

N: A Chinese calligraphic style, created in the Later Han (Eastern Han) period. It is considered the immediate precursor to modern Chinese Characters. (It is sometimes refered to as the "Standard" style)

13. 行書 xíngshū

N: The "Running" Style, a Chinese calligraphic style which attempts to flow in a fashion similar to the "Grass" style but to also retain the clarity of the 楷書 characters.

14. 草書 cǎoshū

N: The "Grass" Style, a Chinese calligraphic style developed from the 隸書 style. This style helped to foster the deve-lopment of 書法 as an art form. Characters are written in a simplistic form which resembles blades of grass and is written very quickly.

15. 印刷體 yìnshuātǐ   *N*: the printed form

16. 正楷 zhèngkǎi

   N: The "Standard" script of modern Chinese calligraphy.
   The form of Chinese characters which you see in books
   (like this textbook).

17. 典雅 diǎnyǎ

   SV: refined; elegant (said of one's writing style, diction,
   etc.)

   那棟建築物看起來很典雅。

   That building was constructed very elegantly (it looks very
   elegant).

18. 辨認 biànrèn   *V*: to recognize; to identify

   這件古物上的字跡模糊，我無法辨認。

   The character markings on this historic relic are blurred; I
   have no way to identify them.

19. 碑銘 bēimíng

   N: a part of an inscriptional writing, usually in rhyme

20. 匾額 biǎné

   N: a (wooden) tablet (usually with an inscription upon it)

21. 題字 tízì   *N/VO*: an inscription

22. 古籍經典 gǔjíjīngdiǎn   *N*: arcient books and classics

   我問他古籍經典，他一臉茫然。

   When I asked him classics, there was uncertainly on his
   face.

23. 旁 páng

N: a lateral radical of a Chinese character (placed either on the right or left side)

「氵」是水旁；「扌」是手旁。

"氵" is the lateral radical for water; "扌" is the lateral radical for hand.

24. 商榷 shāngquè　　*V*: to discuss; to consider; to deliberate

這件事得商榷一下，不可貿然去做。

This matter should be discussed; it should not be done rashly.

25. 神秘 shénmì　　*SV/AT*: to be mysterious; to be mystical

他是個神秘的人，他做的事都很神秘。

He is a mysterious person; what he does is all very mysterious.

二、成語與俗語：Proverbs and Common Sayings:

1. 繼之而起 jìzhīérqǐ

be the successor to; the style, fashion or methodology which follows another

收音機發明之後，繼之而起的是電視。

(The invention) of the television followed that of the radio.

2. 方方正正 fāngfāngzhèngzhèng

to be well-organized; to be perfect; to be well-formed

方方正正的字看起來很整齊。

Well-formed characters look neat.

3. 一筆不苟 yìbǐbùgǒu

(literally: not even one stroke is negligent) to write characters in which every stroke is placed perfectly.

練習書法時，要一筆不苟，才能寫得好。

When studying Chinese calligraphy, one wants to (write characters in such a way that) not even one stroke is negligent, only then can one write well.

4. 龍飛鳳舞 lóngfēifèngwǔ

(literally: with Dragons flying and Phoenixes dancing) To write calligraphy with lively flourishes; to do something with lively flourishes

他寫的字像龍飛鳳舞，很美觀。

He writes characters with lively flourishes; they are very pleasing to the eye.

5. 行雲流水 xíngyúnliúshǔi

(literally: moving clouds and flowing water) to write calligraphy with a very natural and flowing style; to do something with a natural and flowing style

這篇文章如行雲流水。

This essay has a natural and flowing style (it is like moving clouds and flowing water).

三、句型：Sentence Patterns:

1. 自……以後，逐漸……了

since......, ...gradually have......;

from the time of......, ...gradually have become......

(1) 自暑假以後，學生逐漸多了。

(2) 自聖誕節過了以後，買禮物的人逐漸少了。

(3) 自二次世界大戰結束以後，獨立的國家逐漸多了。

2. 竟然……以為……

unexpectedly......, ...believing incorrectly that......;

to one's surprise......, ...thinking wrongly that......

(1) 他竟然生氣了，以為我騙他。

(2) 他竟然辭職了，以為工作很容易找。

(3) 她竟然得意起來，以為每個人都喜歡她。

3. 一般而言……

generally speaking......; in general......

(1) 一般而言，女人的壽命比男人長。

(2) 一般而言，男人的力氣比女人大。

(3) 一般而言，南方人喜歡吃米飯，北方人喜歡吃麵食。

4. 除此以外，尚有……

and besides these......, ...also has......;

aside from these......, ...in addition there is......

(1) 本校有圖書館、運動場，除此以外，尚有游泳池。

(2) 本校的外國學生，有的學會話，有的學作文，除此以外，尚

有人學戲劇。

(3) 今天的晚餐很豐富，有烤鴨、牛排、青菜，除此以外，尚有
龍蝦。

四、易混淆的詞 ： Easily Confused Words:

1. 演變 yǎnbiàn *V/N*: **to develop and change; to evolve**

繁體字演變成簡體字。

The original complex forms of Chinese characters evolved

into the simplified forms of characters.

演進 yǎnjìn

V/N: **to improve through evolutionary process; to develop**

人類是由「猿人」演進而成現在的樣子。

Humans developed from "ape-men" to their present form.

變化 biànhuà

V/N: **to metamorphose; to transform; to transmute**

目前社會結構的變化越來越複雜。

At the moment the structure of society is transforming into

something more and more complex.

2. 實用 shíyòng

AT/SV: **to be practical; to be useful; to be of practical use;**

　　　　　pragmatic

他喜歡買很實用的東西。

He likes to buy very practical things.

實際 shíjì

SV/AT: **an actual situation; an actuality; reality; in practice**

這件事實際上還有很多問題。

This business, in reality, still has a lot of problems.

實ㄕ在ㄗㄞ shízài

A/SV: **really; truly; of a certainty; to be real; to be concrete**

我喜歡實在不虛假的朋友。

I like real, not false friends.

3. 商ㄕㄤ榷ㄑㄩㄝ shāngquè　*V*: **to consider; to deliberate; to discuss**

嚴重的問題該多加仔細商榷。

Serious problems should have additional careful deliberation.

商ㄕㄤ量ㄌㄧㄤ shāngliáng

V: **to exchange opinions or views; to confer; to talk over; to hold a discussion**

這件事情好商量，慢慢談。

This matter is amenable to discussion; let's talk it over slowly.

討ㄊㄠ論ㄌㄨㄣ tǎolùn　*V/N*: **to discuss; a discussion**

經過長時間的討論，大家才決定了這個提案。

After going through a long period of discussion everybody decided on this proposal.

五、問題討論： Questions for Discussion:

1. 簡單說明中國的文字如何演變。

2. 什麼時候中國文字有更大的進步？

_____

3. 請說明通行簡化文字的優點和缺點。

_____

4. 簡字多半是根據什麼而造出的？請舉例說明。

_____

六、角色扮演：Role Playing:

　　一個從臺灣去美國探親的人，和另一個從大陸去美國留學的人，從美國西岸到東岸，在同一機上聊天。對簡字及繁字有不同的看法，開始一場辯論。

七、練習：Practice Exercises:

1. 配句：

Match the Following Phrases to Make Sentences:

(1) 文房四寶：＿＿＿＿　　　A.「乾」和「幹」

(2) 秦始皇：＿＿＿＿　　　B. 有很多碑銘匾額

(3) 楷書(正楷)：＿＿＿＿　　　C. 是筆、墨、紙、硯

(4) 隸書：＿＿＿＿　　　D. 統一中國文字

(5) 簡體字：＿＿＿＿　　　E. 有甲骨文

(6) 名勝古蹟的地方：＿＿＿＿　　　F.「应」

(7) 殷商：＿＿＿＿　　　G. 簡字繁字問題增加了不少困擾

(8)「應」可以寫成：＿＿＿＿　　　H. 方方正正一筆不苟

(9)「干」可以代替：＿＿＿＿　　　I. 減少了不少文盲

⑽ 一旦海峽兩岸正式來往以後：＿＿＿　　　*J.* 在漢朝十分盛行

2. 請辨認簡繁字：

Please Identify and Match the Simplified Characters with Their Complex Counterparts:

⑴ 尘：＿＿＿　　　　　　　　*A.* 幣

⑵ 灭：＿＿＿　　　　　　　　*B.* 塵

⑶ 卫：＿＿＿　　　　　　　　*C.* 發

⑷ 厂：＿＿＿　　　　　　　　*D.* 業

⑸ 币：＿＿＿　　　　　　　　*E.* 滅

⑹ 发：＿＿＿　　　　　　　　*F.* 衛

⑺ 导：＿＿＿　　　　　　　　*G.* 開

⑻ 开：＿＿＿　　　　　　　　*H.* 導

⑼ 关：＿＿＿　　　　　　　　*I.* 廠

⑽ 业：＿＿＿　　　　　　　　*J.* 關

3. 選相似詞：（其中有複選）

Select the Term with the Same Meaning:

＿＿＿⑴工工整整：　*a.*端端正正　*b.*四四方方　*c.*一筆不苟

＿＿＿⑵行雲流水：　*a.*白雲小河　*b.*自然流暢　*c.*方方正正

＿＿＿⑶文盲：　　　*a.*睜眼瞎子　*b.*目不識丁的人　*c.*盲人

＿＿＿⑷比方：　　　*a.*譬喻　　*b.*譬如　　　　*c.*比如

＿＿＿⑸契約：　　　*a.*合約　　*b.*合同　　　　*c.*條約

4. 解釋：

Define the Following Terms:

⑴ 甲骨文：＿＿＿＿＿＿＿＿＿＿＿＿＿＿＿＿＿＿＿＿

⑵ 不可磨滅：＿＿＿＿＿＿＿＿＿＿＿＿＿＿＿＿＿＿＿

(3) 臺灣海峽兩岸：＿＿＿＿＿＿＿＿＿＿＿＿＿＿

(4) 典雅：＿＿＿＿＿＿＿＿＿＿＿＿＿＿＿＿＿＿

(5) 商榷：＿＿＿＿＿＿＿＿＿＿＿＿＿＿＿＿＿＿

佳文欣賞

中國文字的特色

江澄格

中國文字從形音義等構成文字的三要素，分別表現出獨具的特色：

一、**字形方面**：中國文字是由早期的圖畫符號演變而成的象形文字。最初的字形只是寫實的圖畫，如山、川、水、火等；和簡略的符號，如一、二、三；以及形態的標誌，如上、下、凹、凸等。雖經漫長歲月已有不少改變，但至今仍然保留原有的形狀特徵。在字形的組合上，些微的差異，便可顯示出迥然不同的意義，如人、大、太、犬、天、夭、夫、矢、失等筆畫的增減，與部位變動的組合，即能造出涵義不同的新字。晚清《金桂生隨筆》所載沈啟南作的〈詠田字〉短詩，就是以「田」字在字形組合上，部位變動，所表現出不同的字義，也突顯出漢字在字形組合結構上所具有的特性和功能。沈啟南的〈詠田字〉是這樣的：昔日田為「富」字足，今朝田是「累」字頭。拖下腳來成「甲」首，伸出頭去不自「由」。田在心中常「思」量，田放胸中「慮」不休。當初只望田成「福」，誰料田多「疊」成愁。

二、**字音方面**：中國字聲韻分明，一字一音，單音節發音。最大的特色是一個字音，以四聲不同的變化，就能表現出完整的意義，寫

出一篇完整的文章。

三、**字義方面**：中國文字字義明確，詞彙豐富，以有限的單字，可以組合出許多詞彙。中國文字能按照實際的須要，創造出各種不同意義的詞彙來。不像其他的文字，有新的事物發生，就必須另外創造新字才可以下適當的定義。

~節錄自〈歷史文化與藝術的結晶〉《中央日報》~

問答：Answer the following questioin：

1. 就字形來說，中國文字是怎麼演變來的？

_____

2. 請舉例說明在字形的組合上，少許的差異，便可顯示出完全不同的意義。

_____

3. 中國文字在字音方面有什麼特色？

_____

4. 中國文字在字義方面和其他文字有什麼不同？

_____

閱讀與探討
Read and Discuss

簡單介紹中國文字的構造

中國文字的構造方法有六種，叫做六書。

一、象形：照著物體的形象，用筆畫表示出來。

例如：ㅂ（山）、ﾉ（水）、半（牛）、羊（羊）、д（子）
等。

二、指事：用記號表示抽象的事情。

例如：木表示樹，在樹的下面是本本

木 在樹的上面是末

三、會意：合併兩個或兩個以上的字，表示一個新的意思。

例如：「明」是合併日、月二字，表示亮的意思。

「伐」是合併人、戈二字，以表示人拿武器去攻擊的意
思。

「解」是合併刀、牛、角三字，以表示解剖的意思。

四、形聲：由「形符」和「聲符」兩部分結合而成。

例如：晴：青是聲符，日是形符。晴天有太陽。

清：青是聲符，氵是形符。水很清。

五、轉注：因時間地域的不同而造出形體不同的字，但意思相同或
相近，可以互相注釋。

例如：考、老都是年紀大的意思，因此可以用「考，老也。」
「老，考也。」來互相注釋，另外，「問，訊也。」也
是一樣。

六、假借：本來沒有為這個事物造字，就借用與這個事物同音或聲
音相近的字來用。

例如：令：本為發號施令，借為縣令的令。

長：本意是滋長，借用為縣長的長。

有人認為象形、指事、會意、形聲是中國文字構造的方法，而轉
注和假借是中國文字的運用方法。

　　　　　　～節錄自國中《國文》第二冊語文常識，國立編譯館～

練習：指出下列各字屬於象形、指事、會意、假借中的哪一項。

例如：祭—會意　情—形聲　鳥—象形　上—指事

1. 刃： _____

2. 山： _____

3. 魚： _____

4. 弓： _____

5. 下： _____

6. 果： _____

7. 男： _____

8. 忠： _____

9. 信： _____

10. 驚： _____

11. 卡： _____

12. 囚： _____

13. 車： _____

14. 伴： _____

15. 輪： _____

16. 把： _____

17. 江： _____

18. 尖： _____

19. 歪： _____

20. 玲： _____

生詞索引

-T-

-U-

-W-

成語與俗語索引

-R-

-S-

-T-

-W-

-X-

-Y-

-Z-

句型索引

實用視聽華語(三)

主 編 者：國立臺灣師範大學國語教學中心
編輯委員：韓英華・張仲敏・錢進明
策 劃 者：中華民國教育部
著作財產權人：中華民國教育部
發 行 人：武奎煜
出版發行：正中書局
地　　址：台北市衡陽路 20 號
電　　話：(886-2)23822815・23821496
FAX NO：(886-2)23822805
郵政劃撥：0009914-5
http://www.ccbc.com.tw
E-mail: service@ccbc.com.tw
出版日期：西元一九九九年八月臺初版(民88)
　　　　　西元二○○一年一月第二次印行(民90)
版權所有・翻印必究
新聞局出版事業登記證：
局版臺業字第○一九九號 (9756)
分類號碼：802.00.013(3000)(7.8)(版)澤
ISBN　957-09-1236-7

海外分局
香港：集成圖書有限公司
地址：香港九龍油麻地北海街七號地下
電話：(852)23886172-3・FAX NO：(852)23886174
日本：海風書店
地址：東京都千代田區神田神保町一丁目五六番地
電話：(03)32914344・FAX NO：(03)3291-4345
泰國：集成圖書公司
地址：曼谷耀華力路 233 號
電話：2226573・FAX NO：2235483
美國：華強圖書公司
地址：41-35, Kissen Boulevard, Flushing,
　　　N.Y.11355 U.S.A.
電話：(718)7628889・FAX NO：(718)7628889
歐洲：英華圖書公司
地址：14, Gerrard Street, London, WIV 7LJ
電話：(0171) 4398825・FAX NO：(0171) 4391183

定　價：四三○元

國家圖書館出版品預行編目資料

實用視聽華語／國立臺灣師範大學國語教學中
心主編．－－臺初版．－－臺北市：正中，民
88

　　冊：　公分．
　ISBN 957-09-1237-5(第一冊:平裝)．--
ISBN 957-09-1238-3(第二冊上:平裝)．--
ISBN 957-09-1239-1(第二冊下:平裝)．--
ISBN 957-09-1236-7(第三冊:平裝)

1.中國語言 - 讀本
802.86　　　　　　　　　　　　88006350